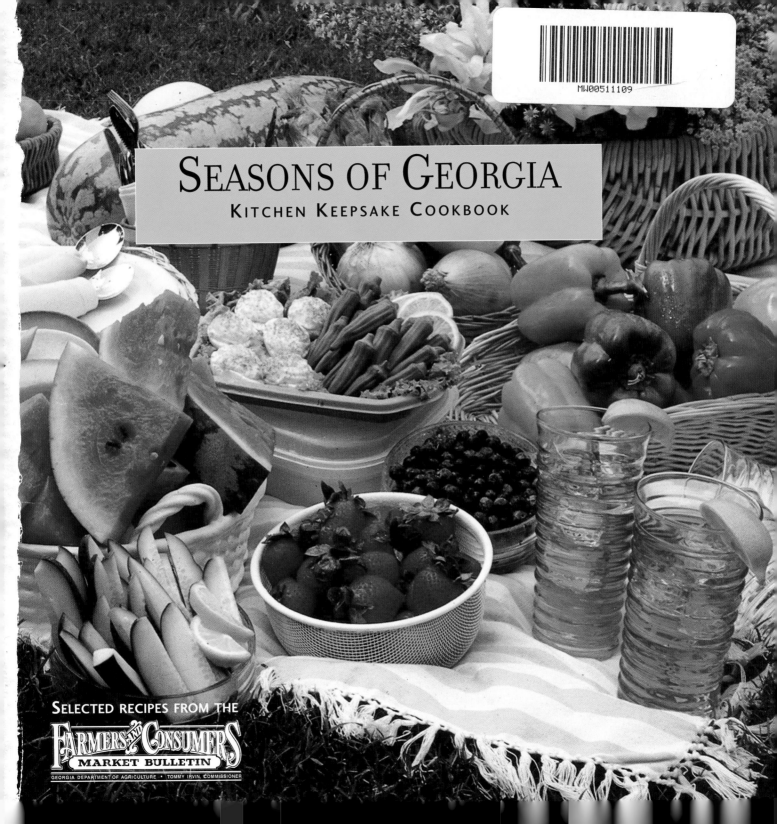

SEASONS OF GEORGIA

KITCHEN KEEPSAKE COOKBOOK

SELECTED RECIPES FROM THE

FARMERS AND CONSUMERS
MARKET BULLETIN

GEORGIA DEPARTMENT OF AGRICULTURE • TOMMY IRVIN, COMMISSIONER

MW00511109

SEASONS OF GEORGIA

KITCHEN KEEPSAKE COOKBOOK

GEORGIA DEPARTMENT OF AGRICULTURE • TOMMY IRVIN, COMMISSIONER

The Georgia Department of Agriculture

PHOENIX MEDIA
NETWORK, INC.

PHOTO CREDITS:

COVER PHOTO: Georgia Department of Agriculture — Parallax Digital, Kennesaw, Georgia
TABLE OF CONTENTS: p. 6-7 StockFood — The Food Image Agency
SPRING: pg.17 Vidalia Onion Committee; pg. 18 Georgia Pecan Commission; pg. 19, 23 National Pork Board; pg. 20 Georgia Peach Commission;
  pg. 21, 22 StockFood — The Food Image Agency
SUMMER: pg. 25 Georgia Peach Commission; pg. 28 National Watermelon Board; pg. 29 Catfish Institute;
  pg. 26, 27, 30, 31, 32 StockFood — The Food Image Agency
FALL: pg. 33 Georgia Apple Commission; pg. 34, 36, 38, 39 StockFood — The Food Image Agency
WINTER: pg. 41 Georgia Pecan Commission; pg. 43 National Pork Board; pg. 42, 44, 46, 48 StockFood — The Food Image Agency

GEORGIA DEPARTMENT OF AGRICULTURE
Tommy Irvin, Commissioner
Marcia Crowley, Agriculture Manager
Helen Sturgeon, Home Economist
Harvey Robertson, Distribution and Marketing
Carlton Moore, Editor, *Farmers and Consumers Market Bulletin*

PHOENIX MEDIA NETWORK. INC.
Jim Prevor, President
Ken Whitacre, Publisher
Jan Fialkow, Managing Editor
E. Shaunn Alderman, Contributing Editor
Jacqueline Tucker, Graphic Designer
Diana Levine, Production Director
Ellen Beth Rosenthal, Photo Assistant

ISBN-13: 978-0-9773225-0-3
ISBN-10: 0-9773225-0-5

Printed in the United States of America
First Printing, February 2007

Preface

Tommy Irvin

Growing up on a farm opens your eyes to many things, including the beauty of nature, the harshness of weather and the goodness of the earth. Farm life builds solid foundations and teaches us life's many lessons.

Our bountiful state, with its mild climate, ample rainfall and rich soils, produces an impressive assortment of fruits and vegetables. We're known for our chicken and other livestock, but consumers also savor seafood from our Atlantic coast. From our fragrant peach orchards and dusty peanut fields to our shady pecan groves and blazing rows of corn, Georgia provides us many outstanding reasons to give thanks.

I've lived long and well since 1956 when I was elected to my first public office as a member of the Habersham County Board of Education. I've experienced much during the past 50 years of service, and one constant has been the enjoyment of good food. Whether it's been cobblers filled with berries fresh off the vines or beans from a backyard garden, I've enjoyed Georgia Grown products. I have happy memories of delicious meals prepared by my mother on our farm in north Georgia. The food was picked fresh, cooked with tenderness and served with love.

The next time you cook up a pot of greens, bake an apple pie or shuck ears of corn, think about Georgia farmers and their families. Farmers are strategists when planning crops and calculating yields. They are weather-watchers who function at the mercy of the elements. They are risk- takers who are often under-appreciated. Let's be grateful for their vision, dedication and effort.

Cooking from this collection of recipes submitted from the heart by readers of the *Farmers and Consumers Market Bulletin* will help you build lasting memories. Involve your family and share your pleasure for our state's wonderful products. You don't have to grow up on a farm to appreciate the goodness of food. My wife Bernice and I have five children, 14 grandchildren and one great-grandchild. There are a lot of stories there and we know how children like to create in the kitchen.

I hope you will enjoy serving friends and family using recipes from this *Seasons of Georgia* cookbook.

Tommy Irvin

Commissioner
Georgia Department of Agriculture

THIS BOOK IS DEDICATED TO THE LOYAL STAFF AND EMPLOYEES OF THE GEORIGIA DEPARTMENT OF AGRICULTURE AS WELL AS THE FAITHFUL READERS OF THE FARMERS AND CONSUMERS MARKET BULLETIN

TABLE OF CONTENTS

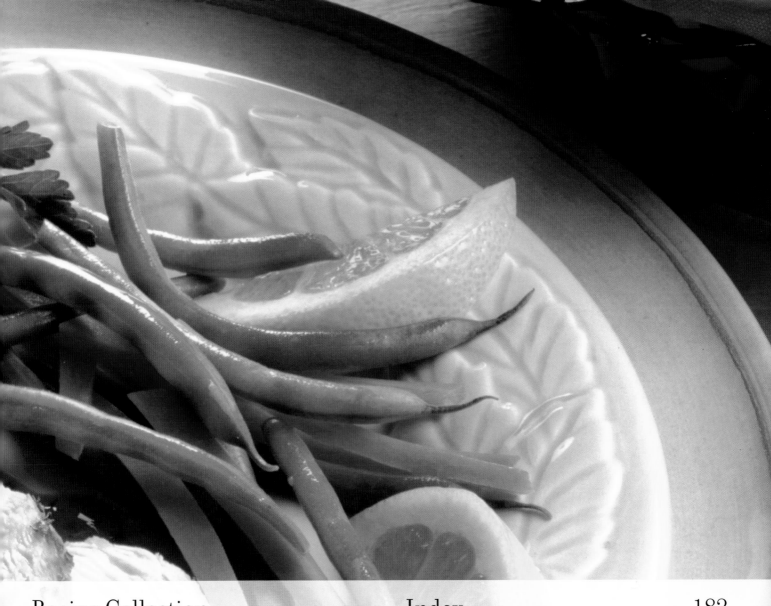

Recipe Collection

Acknowledgements

Seasons of Georgia: Kitchen Keepsake Cookbook is no ordinary cookbook. The recipes weren't whipped up by a celebrity, nobody produced a TV show, and we are not planning on opening a restaurant in Vegas. Instead, the vast majority of recipes in this cookbook are tried-and-true recipes used by individual families in the state of Georgia. Many of the recipes were tested with sons and daughters, moms and dads, uncles, aunts, grandmas and grandpas. It was around tables burgeoning with the dishes highlighted in this book that good friends laughed, courting couples flirted, and, in sad times, more than a few tears were shed.

So the very first acknowledgement we give is to the readers of the *Farmers and Consumers Market Bulletin*, which, for almost a century, has been the newsletter of the Georgia Department of Agriculture.

Today's hot culinary trends involve the use of locally grown, fresh ingredients and cuisines reflective of the authentic local culture. Well, guess what? The *Market Bulletin* readers were doing "local," "fresh" and "authentic" well before anyone declared it "cool." In this recipe repository, we have a priceless gift, and it is our pride and pleasure to make this cookbook available to a wider audience.

The man without whom this cookbook would not be possible is Tommy Irvin, Georgia Commissioner of Agriculture since 1969. Commissioner Irvin is the dean of Georgia's constitutional officers. It is his expansive vision for the place that food grown and produced in Georgia can serve in the culinary world that animates this book.

His team at the Georgia Department of Agriculture, including Assistant Commissioner Bobby Harris and the department's marketing division, particularly staff member Marcia Crowley, contributed to the making of this book. Carlton Moore, Editor of *Farmers and Consumers Market Bulletin*, also lent his help. All have a passion for spreading the word about Georgia's unique and diverse agricultural products.

The man who played the vital role of liaison between the public concerns of the department and the private world of publishing and printing was Harvey Robertson, who not only arranged for the execution of this book, but also played an important role in its design, conceptualization and overall look and feel. There was never a more ardent advocate of making this book reader-friendly and a true "Kitchen Keepsake."

Marcia Crowley, who is the department's Agriculture Manager, and Helen Sturgeon, who is a home economist and the chief recipe tester for all of the department's recipes, are the true masterminds behind the selection and organization of the recipes in this book. Listening to these two experts speak to one another and watching them work together was like sitting in the front row of a great symphony.

Marcia and Helen have both cooked and tasted all of the recipes in this book. Not only did they have an intimate knowledge of the recipes, but they also communicated an overall "feel" for the way the recipes should be organized and how these recipes fit into the southern meal. The menus you will read are a result of their careful consideration and deep concern that the reader should have a wonderful experience when cooking and eating the dishes we feature in this cookbook.

On the production side of actually putting the pages together, Managing Editor Jan Fialkow, who is an expert cook in her own right and experienced editor of recipes/cookbooks, gets credit for getting all the I's dotted and the T's crossed. Her eye for graphic design also came in handy when selecting photographs and supervising our photo shoots.

Contributing Editor E. Shaunn Alderman was also an integral part of the editorial team. Shaunn's southern-belle charm and sentiment can be witnessed in all the introductory pages of the recipe section. Her advice and counsel in making this book a true keepsake is perhaps spawned out of her own southern heritage and desire to chronicle her memories and pass this book on to her children.

The beautiful pages and overall graphic treatment of this book are the result of the talents of Jacqueline Tucker. Her hard work and devotion to getting each page designed perfectly are most appreciated.

Diana Levine, Production Director, took charge of bringing this labor of love into printable form. Without Diana's vast knowledge in print production, this book would not have been the same.

In addition, I would like to thank Ellen B. Rosenthal, my assistant (and capable photo stylist), as well as my own family — especially my wife, Kerry — for their advice and counsel on this book. Ellen and Kerry both created many of the dishes from the recipes in this book, and I had the pleasure of eating the dishes along the way.

Finally, the man who ultimately made this all possible on the publishing and printing side of *Seasons of Georgia* is my business partner, Jim Prevor. Jim's early vision for the concept and content of the book has made this a better, more important book than it might have otherwise been. His business acumen has made it all possible.

Famous 19th century British Prime Minister, Benjamin Disraeli, once wrote, "The best way to become acquainted with a subject is to write a book about it." In the case of producing this book, I can vouch for that observation. Reading each recipe, conversing with the experts at the department, doing research on Georgia and southern cooking, shooting the photos, and, of course, tasting the dishes, all were a wonderful experience.

I know you will get as much pleasure out of using this book as we did in creating it.

Ken Whitacre
Publisher

Introduction

Over the years, loyal readers of the *Farmers and Consumers Market Bulletin* have proven to be wonderful southern cooks. Your willingness to share your favorite recipes has given us a sizeable file of tried-and-true traditional recipes as well as some delicious "new South" style dishes. It is our pleasure to compile a variety of those recipes (and a few other favorites) into this new cookbook, *Seasons of Georgia*.

Our staff tested (and tasted) all of the recipes in this cookbook, so you can be assured that they are all special. We revised some slightly, lightened some up and even renamed a few, but the basic intention was preserved — to provide you and your family with a good variety of "home-style" southern recipes using Georgia-grown products season by season.

We have provided tips and suggestions alongside many of the recipes. In addition, there are spaces in this book where we encourage you to write your memories of learning to cook, events surrounding certain types of recipes or even your favorite version of our recipe. We hope your additions will make this a book your children and grandchildren will cherish for years to come.

Helen Sturgeon
Home Economist

About This Book

Food can comfort us physically, but even more important, it can comfort us emotionally. The preparation and memories associated with certain dishes can be nurturing and even inspirational. Sitting down to the favorite meal or the special dish of a loved one can provide a bridge to the past or a link to some far-off location.

While this is not a how-to book about cooking, we hope *Seasons of Georgia: Kitchen Keepsake Cookbook* will inspire you to try new tastes you have not yet experienced and enjoy old favorite recipes you may have forgotten. We encourage you to embellish the pages with your own cooking tips, family stories and favorite recipes. Your thoughtful hints and anecdotes will inspire and entertain others who read your handwritten remarks in years to come.

For many people, cooking and enjoying food is similar to crafting scrapbooks, which is a popular way to preserve, share and pass along memories. Whether a baby's first curl is saved with a tiny ribbon or great grandfather's railroad photos are treasured, family history can be cherished by reminiscing over decorated pages. Through food, stories can be told, history revealed, occasions celebrated and love shared.

Sharing food opens the world, creates opportunity and may bring peace during turmoil. The simple act of sharing is a meaningful lesson children learn by observation. We can ask our children or grand-

children for help in the kitchen when preparing a meal for a friend in need. The hands-on cooking experience can create a lifelong memory and establish your family's position about caring for others.

Food can be a substitute for words when we don't know a language or what words to use. Many neighbors have met because someone baked a pie or cake and made a thoughtful delivery. Have you ever introduced yourself to new neighbors by baking a treat to welcome them? Do you still know those neighbors today?

Memories can be created with food or conjured by food. All the senses are involved and stimulated when we are cooking. Have you ever smelled biscuits baking and relived a memory where biscuits are the main focus? Our minds can barely resist thinking of past holiday meals when presented with the delicious aroma of roasting turkey.

Cooking also invokes joy. We confess to past kitchen failures by justifying that the dish was "only a little burnt." Laughter follows, and usually more stories are told. Do you have kitchen confessions you would like to share? Remember, experience is a significant teacher, and laughter is great medicine!

In a gesture to keep the music playing, a banjo player may arrange for his banjo to one day be passed along to a relative or friend. The strings will be strummed, songs will be sung and memories of the original owner celebrated.

In a cook's kitchen, good pots and pans are often passed down from one generation to the next. A well-seasoned cast iron skillet is a symbolic and valued inheritance. The gift is a way of encouraging the recipient to keep on cooking. We can be sure recipes are gifted to the next generation as well.

Many recipes are not written down but passed along by preparing them together. Unlike earlier generations, many families today live far apart, so the opportunities to cook together are not as numerous. This means some family recipes could be lost or forgotten. What are your oldest family recipes and where do you keep them? Perhaps some recipes in this book will jog your memory of an old family favorite and inspire you to write the recipe down.

From coffee and cocoa to party punch and flavored iced tea, we Southerners are quite fond of a variety of beverages. The absence of beverage recipes in this cookbook is simple to explain: We needed more pages. Yes, we could have held back on a few dessert recipes or perhaps reduced the number of main dishes, but the decision was made to shine the spotlight on the food rather than the drink.

No doubt recipe contributors across the South will continue serving their favorite drinks when they prepare recipes from *Seasons of Georgia*. Are you known for making a particular party punch or a hot holiday brew? Consider writing the recipes in this book and sharing serving tips. Your additions will tailor the menus we offer and help create a more customized recipe collection for your family.

Georgians should feel appreciative about life's many blessings, including a bountiful state rich

with agricultural products, thriving industries and interesting history. Whether we are tailgating in a stadium parking lot, picnicking in a beautiful park or taking a covered dish to a church supper, we like to celebrate! *Seasons of Georgia* offers recipes from Southerners who enjoy food, family and traditions. The recipes are comforting and enticing. Preparing the dishes will help us commemorate special occasions, carry us through difficult days and inspire us to share our passion for cooking with family and friends.

We encourage you to personalize this collection by writing notes throughout the book and including helpful hints you've learned through the years. Space in the back of the book will enable you to make this collection a recipe keepsake worthy of passing along. You may even consider attaching a few cherished photographs taken during shared family meals. Your thoughtful notes, recipes and additions will nurture and inspire the next generation of cooks.

Best wishes to you as you prepare, taste and share the recipes from *Seasons of Georgia: Kitchen Keepsake Cookbook*.

E. Shaunn Alderman
Contributing Editor

Seasonal Menus

SPRING

SUMMER

FALL

WINTER

SPRING

Spring is the season when nature graciously offers a colorful invitation to rejoice. Georgia hillsides are delicately illuminated with blooming dogwood trees, and sweet, golden jonquils pop up along wooded paths. We host engagement parties and graduation celebrations while regarding additional occasions worthy of commemoration. The mild-weather season dappled with inspiring colors sets the tone for entertaining and celebrating.

Whether planning a bridal shower, baptism luncheon or retirement reception, we can easily include dishes from this recipe collection to enhance our gatherings. These suggested menus for an Easter Dinner, Mother's Day Brunch, Ladies Luncheon and Anniversary Reception will ease the planning process and enable us to focus on the reason for celebrating.

Inviting guests when we prepare Vidalia Onion Pie, Quick Blueberry Muffins or Apple Chicken Salad is not essential, but guests will be gratified — spring in Georgia justifies every invitation. Embellish these menus with your own family favorites or use the menus as a way to divide cooking duties among co-hosts. Sharing time in the kitchen with people we care about is another way to sweeten the taste of the event and the food.

Mother's Day Brunch

BREAKFAST CASSEROLE *(Pg. 121)*

VIDALIA ONION PIE *(Pg. 61)*

GRAPE SALAD *(Pg. 82)*

**CRUNCHY GREEN BEANS
WITH PECANS** *(Pg. 109)*

LUSCIOUS LEMON SQUARES *(Pg. 172)*

Breakfast Casserole

Ladies' Luncheon

APPLE CHICKEN SALAD *(Pg. 76)*

LAYERED VEGETABLE SALAD *(Pg. 82)*

OR

COLD VEGETABLE SOUP *(Pg. 94)*

BLUEBERRY MUFFINS *(Pg. 67)*

INDIVIDUAL PEACH CHEESECAKES *(Pg. 170)*

OR

CHERRY FLUFF *(Pg. 154)*

Cold Vegetable Soup

Easter Dinner

BAKED HAM *(Pg. 119)*

SOUR CREAM POTATO SALAD *(Pg. 85)*

ROASTED ASPARAGUS *(Pg. 114)*

CARROT SOUFFLÉ *(Pg. 105)*

SOUR CREAM PECAN POUND CAKE *(Pg. 177)*

Baked Ham

Anniversary Reception

PECAN CHEESE CRACKERS *(Pg. 56)*

CHEESE STRAWS *(Pg. 51)*

SMOKED SALMON PECAN SPREAD *(Pg. 59)*

MAKE-AHEAD ROLL-UP SANDWICHES *(Pg. 54)*

**ASSORTED FRUIT AND
VEGETABLE TRAYS** *(No recipe)*

**CHOCOLATE ITALIAN CREAM CAKE WITH
CHOCOLATE CREAM CHEESE FROSTING**
(Pg. 156)

SUMMER

Summer in the Peach State might be the most memory-making season. There are picnics at the lake, beach vacations, weddings, family reunions and weekends spent in the mountains. Bountiful summer gardens often inspire us to recreate flavors we have savored in the past. Whether we use our own backyard tomatoes, green beans and squash, or peaches and watermelon from a roadside stand, Georgia produce has a starring role in the summertime.

As Georgia was one of the original 13 colonies, we rightly claim to be a patriotic group that makes no excuses for our many gatherings. Bringing friends and family together with a cookout is a popular way we make the most of summer. Casual entertaining is at its peak when the grill is hot and relaxed guests are enjoying great food. These suggested menus for a Father's Day Cook Out, Fish Fry, July 4th Barbecue and Family Reunion will make it easier when planning summer events.

We all have childhood memories that take us back to long-ago summers. A fishing trip with Grandpa turned more memorable when the day's catch became the evening's meal. A peach-picking outing, hot as it was, developed into a kitchen adventure when Grandma showed us how to make a delicious cobbler. Summer in Georgia is ripe for reminiscing, and it's the ideal season to make new memories.

Father's Day Cook Out

EASY LONDON BROIL *(Pg. 129)*

**GREEN CHILE CHEESE
CORN CASSEROLE** *(Pg. 111)*

WARM GRAPE TOMATOES *(Pg. 116)*

**CRUNCHY GREEN BEANS WITH
CARAMELIZED VIDALIA ONIONS** *(Pg. 108)*

LEMON CHESS PIE *(Pg. 171)*
OR
ICE CREAM SANDWICH DESSERT *(Pg. 168)*

Easy London Broil

Fish Fry

**CRISP FRIED CATFISH
WITH REMOULADE SAUCE** *(Pg. 128)*

EGGPLANT PROVENÇAL *(Pg. 110)*

GOLDEN HUSH PUPPIES *(Pg. 70)*

SLAW *(No recipe)*

WATERMELON SALSA *(Pg. 62)*

PEACH COBBLER *(Pg. 174)*

Crisp Fried Catfish

July 4th Barbecue

LOW AND SLOW PULLED PORK *(Pg. 132)*

APPLE BARBECUED RIBS *(Pg. 118)*

CHUNKY VEGETABLE SALAD *(Pg. 79)*

CORN ON THE COB *(No recipe)*

SLICED HOME GROWN TOMATOES *(No recipe)*

HOMEMADE BLUEBERRY ICE CREAM *(Pg. 168)*

WATERMELON *(No recipe)*

Apple Barbecued Ribs

Family Reunion

BUTTERMILK FRIED CHICKEN *(Pg. 122)*

COPPER PENNIES *(Pg. 79)*

FESTIVE PASTA SALAD *(Pg. 81)*

COMPANY SQUASH CASSEROLE *(Pg. 108)*

**RICH AND DELICIOUS
BANANA PUDDING** *(Pg. 177)*

**CHOCOLATE SHEET CAKE
WITH CHOCOLATE FROSTING** *(Pg. 159)*

FALL

We can't count on the weather to signal the arrival of fall in Georgia because warm conditions often are long lasting. We know it's fall when cotton fields are harvested and pumpkin patches sporting scarecrows crop up along country roads. But before the hayrides and the changing color of leaves, we know the season has turned into fall when tailgating begins. Flavors of fall in Georgia include pre-game snacks and delicacies devoured in stadium parking lots across the state.

Hunting season is another indicator. A first fall hunt may be followed by a traditional hearty breakfast — a tasty way to welcome the season and reward the hunters. These suggested menus for a Tailgate Party, Hearty Fall Breakfast, Covered Dish Dinner and Thanksgiving Dinner will motivate us to create new tastes and welcome a season that seems both revitalizing and relaxing.

Though autumn vegetables are not forgotten, fall festivals around the state shine attention on Georgia apples. Sweet or tart, red, golden or green, Georgia apples are revered when cooks create with them. Whether we buy apples at festivals or we visit nearby orchards for a U-pick experience, apples are a delicious part of fall in Georgia.

Tailgate Party

GRILLED LEMON AND OREGANO CHICKEN BREASTS *(Pg. 129)*

CHICKEN DRUMMETTES *(Pg. 51)*

ZUCCHINI SQUARES *(Pg. 62)*

ASSORTED CHIPS AND DIPS *(No recipe)*

DOUBLE CHOCOLATE BROWNIES *(Pg. 163)*

Double Chocolate Brownies

Hearty Fall Breakfast

COUNTRY HAM AND RED EYE GRAVY
(No recipe)

CHEESE GRITS *(Pg. 107)*

SAUTÉED APPLES AND BACON *(Pg. 114)*

SWEET POTATO BISCUITS *(Pg. 74)*
OR
BASIC BUTTERMILK BISCUITS *(Pg. 65)*

BANANA BREAD *(Pg. 64)*

Sautéed Apples And Bacon

Thanksgiving Dinner

TRADITIONAL TURKEY AND DRESSING *(No recipe)*

OR

HERBED TURKEY BREAST *(Pg. 130)*

LOW-FAT BROCCOLI RICE CASSEROLE *(Pg. 112)*

CRANBERRY SALAD *(Pg. 80)*

SPOON ROLLS *(Pg. 73)*

TRADITIONAL PECAN PIE *(Pg. 181)*

Herbed Turkey Breast

Covered Dish Dinner

CHICKEN AND MUSHROOM TETRAZZINI *(Pg. 125)*

SOUTHERN SHEPARD'S PIE WITH CORNBREAD DRESSING *(Pg. 145)*

POTATO CASSEROLE *(Pg. 113)*

FIG CAKE WITH BUTTERMILK GLAZE *(Pg. 164)*

STRAWBERRY-PINEAPPLE DESSERT *(Pg. 179)*

WINTER

Winter rains may wash in the season, but nothing can dampen the tradition of focusing on home and family during Georgia winters. December is filled with planning, preparation and presentation as Christmas nears. While we are decorating our homes, we are often baking for cookie exchanges or making tasty gifts for teachers and friends. Sharing food is a thoughtful way to spread the spirit of the season.

Inviting prosperity and luck for the New Year by serving greens and black-eye peas on January 1st is a long-followed Southern tradition. But there's no harm in adding a twist to an old tradition. These suggested menus for a Christmas Dinner, New Year's Day Lunch, "Souper" Bowl Sunday and Valentine's Dessert are enticing and satisfying. As much as we enjoy cooking favorites of the past, we also like trying new tastes.

Georgia is the Number One pecan-producing state in the nation. It's a good thing the state annually produces 88 millions pounds of pecans, because we include pecans in our breakfasts, lunches and dinners. And, of course, we snack on them — whether they are sweet or savory.

Winter is a cozy time for creating in the kitchen. Testing new recipes using Georgia pecans is a sure way to achieve flavorful results.

Christmas Dinner

**SINFULLY DELICIOUS
SUGARED PECANS** *(Pg. 58)*

**MARINATED PORK LOIN
WITH HOLIDAY SAUCE** *(Pg. 135)*

WILD RICE *(No recipe)*

**CRUNCHY GREEN BEANS
WITH ROSEMARY, PECANS AND LEMON**
(Pg. 109)

**BREAD PUDDING
WITH LEMON SAUCE** *(Pg. 152)*

Marinated Pork Loin

New Year's Day Lunch

TURNIP GREEN CASSEROLE *(Pg. 116)*

BLACK-EYE PEA CAVIAR *(Pg. 50)*

ASSORTED SAUSAGES *(No recipe)*

SOUTHERN STYLE
BUTTERMILK CORNBREAD *(Pg. 73)*

Black-Eye Pea Caviar

"Souper" Bowl Sunday

CHILI CREOLE *(Pg. 93)*

EASY BRUNSWICK STEW *(Pg. 95)*

SPICY CHICKEN SOUP *(Pg. 100)*

HEARTY VEGETABLE SOUP *(Pg. 96)*

ASSORTED BREADS AND CRACKERS *(No recipe)*

Hearty Vegetable Soup

Valentine's Dessert

CHOCOLATE RASPBERRY CAKE *(Pg. 158)*

CHEESECAKE *(Pg. 154)*

CHOCOLATE SNICKER PIE *(Pg. 160)*

**STRAWBERRY CAKE
WITH STRAWBERRY FROSTING** *(Pg. 178)*

Recipe Collection

APPETIZERS AND SNACKS

Southern hospitality dictates that hosts will graciously be ready for impromptu entertaining. Having goodies on hand in the freezer for quick thawing and a well-stocked pantry is the best way to welcome guests no matter their arrival time. This enticing selection of Appetizers and Snacks offers an A to Z range of gratifying choices.

From Hot Artichoke Dip *(pg. 52)* to Zucchini Squares *(pg. 62)*, you will find many flavors to enjoy. Cheese Straws *(pg. 51)* and Sinfully Delicious Sugared Pecans *(pg. 58)* are ideal to nibble on while rocking on a front porch. Ready to taste beyond the classics? Try Roasted Nut Chicken Pâté *(pg. 57)* and Smoked Salmon Pecan Spread *(pg. 59)*. Many claim the best Watermelon Salsa *(pg. 62)* is made with Georgia watermelons. Whether hosting a special occasion party or tailgating before a big game, these recipes will help you create memorable tastes to be savored for years.

Appetizer Muffins

YIELD: *24 miniature muffins*

2	sticks butter, melted
2	cups self-rising flour
1	cup sour cream

Preheat oven to 400°.

Combine ingredients in medium bowl; stir gently. Drop by tablespoons into lightly greased miniature muffin pans.

Bake for 12 to 15 minutes.

Black-Eye Pea Caviar (PICTURED ON PAGE 45)

Doris H. Davis
Ft. Valley, Georgia

YIELD: *6 cups*

2	16-ounce cans black-eye peas, rinsed and drained
1	16-ounce can white hominy, rinsed and drained
2	large jalapeño peppers, seeded and diced
2	large tomatoes, chopped
1	medium Vidalia onion, chopped
1	medium green pepper, chopped
1	tablespoon sugar
1	teaspoon salt
½ - 1	teaspoon ground black pepper
½	teaspoon dried dill weed
1	tablespoon olive oil
2	tablespoons balsamic vinegar
	Tortilla chips

Mix all ingredients except tortilla chips in large bowl. Refrigerate overnight to allow flavors to blend. Serve with tortilla chips.

VARIATIONS: Substitute ½ to ⅔ cup mayonnaise for the balsamic vinegar and olive oil.

Substitute whole kernel corn for hominy and 3 tablespoons fresh cilantro for dill weed.

Substitute black beans for some or all of the black-eye peas.

"We ate the 'original' in a huge steak restaurant in Amarillo, Texas. It was served with chips while we waited for our steaks. They probably used more jalapeños than I do! You can make it as hot as you like."

—Doris Davis

CHEESE STRAWS (PICTURED ON PAGE 24)

YIELD: *Approximately 4 dozen*

1½	cups all-purpose flour
¼	teaspoon salt
¼	teaspoon baking powder
¼	teaspoon dry mustard
	Ground red pepper to taste (start with ¼ teaspoon and work up)
	Garlic salt to taste (about ½ teaspoon)
1	stick margarine or butter, very cold
1	cup grated extra sharp Cheddar cheese

Preheat oven to 350°.

Place dry ingredients in food processor bowl fitted with metal blade. Cut cold butter into tablespoons and drop into food processor while machine is running; process until ingredients are well blended. Add grated cheese and process until mixture forms stiff dough.

Place dough in cookie press; press dough in desired shape onto ungreased baking sheet. Bake for 10 minutes or until light golden brown. Place on wax paper to cool completely before storing in airtight container.

This recipe doubles easily. Freeze extras for up to 6 months.

Sara T. Dukes
Bartow, Georgia

CHICKEN DRUMMETTES

YIELD: *34 appetizer servings*

3	pounds chicken drummettes (about 34)
½	teaspoon garlic powder
½	cup chicken broth
⅓	cup soy sauce
3	tablespoon sugar
3	tablespoons light brown sugar
3	tablespoons vinegar
¼	teaspoon ground ginger

Preheat oven to 325°.

Place chicken in baking pan. Sprinkle with garlic powder.

Combine remaining ingredients in small bowl; stir until well blended. Pour over chicken, cover, and refrigerate overnight or several hours.

Bake uncovered for 2 hours. Serve warm.

GARDEN APPETIZER PIZZA

YIELD: *30 squares*

2	8-count packages refrigerated crescent rolls
1	8-ounce package cream cheese, softened
½	cup mayonnaise
2	teaspoons dried dill weed
1 ½	teaspoons garlic salt
¼	cup milk
½	cup chopped broccoli
½	cup chopped green onions
1	cup chopped tomatoes
½	cup chopped black olives
½	cup chopped green pepper
½	cup chopped red bell pepper

Preheat oven to 375°.

Unroll dough and spread onto lightly greased 10x15-inch baking pan; press edges and perforations to seal. Bake for 11 minutes. Cool to room temperature.

Combine cream cheese, mayonnaise, dill weed and garlic salt in small bowl; mix well. Add enough milk to make spreading consistency. Spread over crust. Sprinkle vegetables over cream cheese layer. Cut into squares to serve.

HOT ARTICHOKE DIP

YIELD: *2 ½ cups*

1	14-ounce can artichoke hearts, drained and chopped
1	cup mayonnaise
1	cup grated Parmesan cheese
½	teaspoon garlic powder
	Assorted crackers

Preheat oven to 350°.

Combine all ingredients in a medium mixing bowl, stirring to combine. Spoon into a lightly greased 3-quart baking dish. Bake for 20 minutes. Serve warm with assorted crackers.

Also great with crudités. Offer an assortment of colorful cut vegetables, such as carrot and celery sticks, or radish and broccoli bites, for those nibblers cutting back on crackers.

HOT CHEESY BEEF DIP

YIELD: *1 1/2 cups*

1/3	cup chopped Georgia pecans
1	tablespoon melted butter
1	8-ounce package cream cheese, softened
2	tablespoons milk
1	2 1/2-ounce jar dried beef, finely chopped
1/4	cup finely chopped green pepper
1/4	cup finely chopped green onion
1	clove garlic, minced
1/2	teaspoon white pepper
1/2	cup sour cream
	Assorted crackers

Preheat oven to 350°.

Sauté pecans in butter 3 to 5 minutes; drain on paper towels and set aside.

Combine cream cheese and milk in medium mixing bowl; beat on medium speed of electric mixer until smooth. Stir in chopped beef, green pepper, green onion, garlic and white pepper. Stir in sour cream; spoon into a greased 1-quart baking dish. Sprinkle pecans on top and bake for 25 minutes. Serve dip hot with assorted crackers.

HOT CRAB SPREAD

YIELD: *1 1/2 cups*

1	8-ounce package cream cheese, softened
1	6-ounce can crabmeat, drained
2	tablespoons sherry
2	tablespoons horseradish
	Dash Worcestershire sauce
	Assorted cocktail bread or crackers

Preheat oven to 350°.

Combine all ingredients in a small mixing bowl; stir to combine. Spoon into a lightly greased 1-quart baking dish. Bake for 30 minutes. Serve warm with cocktail bread or crackers.

LAYERED NACHO DIP

YIELD: *6 cups*

1	16-ounce can refried beans
1/2	1.25-ounce package taco seasoning mix
1	6-ounce container refrigerated avocado dip
1	8-ounce container sour cream
1	14 1/2-ounce can chopped ripe olives, drained
2	large tomatoes, chopped
1	small onion, chopped
1	4-ounce can chopped green chiles, drained
1 1/2	cups (6-ounces) shredded Mexican cheese
	Tortilla chips

Combine beans and seasoning mix; spread evenly in serving dish. Layer remaining ingredients in order listed. Serve with tortilla chips.

Grandchildren visiting? They love projects. Try turning this lunchtime treat into a hands-on kitchen experience all of you will remember.

MAKE-AHEAD ROLL-UP SANDWICHES

YIELD: *40 pinwheel sandwiches*

4	10-inch flour tortillas
4	tablespoons ranch salad dressing
24	slices deli ham or turkey
12	slices cheese (American, Monterey Jack, Muenster, Swiss or Provolone)
2	cups shredded lettuce

Place tortillas on a cutting board; spread each tortilla with 1 tablespoon salad dressing, spreading to edges. Top each tortilla with 6 slices deli meat, 3 slices cheese and 1/2 cup lettuce, covering the entire surface. Repeat with remaining ingredients.

Roll each tortilla jelly roll fashion. Wrap tightly in plastic wrap. Refrigerate 30 minutes or overnight. When ready to serve, cut into 1-inch slices.

PECAN BLUE CHEESE SPREAD

YIELD: *1 1/2 cups*

1	8-ounce package cream cheese, softened
4	ounces crumbled blue cheese
1/4	teaspoon ground nutmeg
1/4	teaspoon paprika
1/4	teaspoon ground red pepper
1	tablespoon grated onion
2	teaspoons Worcestershire sauce
1	teaspoon lemon juice
1/4	cup chopped and toasted Georgia pecans
	Fresh parsley, chopped
	Assorted crackers

Combine first 8 ingredients in large bowl of food processor; process until smooth.

Line a medium mixing bowl with plastic wrap; spread pecans over bottom of bowl. Spoon cream cheese mixture over pecan layer. Cover with plastic wrap and refrigerate overnight.

Invert onto serving dish to serve. Remove plastic wrap and garnish with chopped parsley. Serve with assorted crackers.

Do you have favorite recipes using blue cheese? Is there a family recipe for a favorite cheese spread? Consider writing notes or recipes on this page for the next generation.

Georgia Pecan
Commission

Great gift idea! When you want to take something homemade to a friend, neighbor or party host, remember how easy these delicious crackers are to make and how convenient they are to take.

PECAN CHEESE CRACKERS

YIELD: *6 dozen*

1	pound shredded sharp Cheddar cheese
1	cup butter or margarine, softened
3	cups self-rising flour
½	teaspoon cayenne pepper
2	cups finely chopped Georgia pecans

Preheat oven to 350°.

Combine cheese and butter in large bowl of electric mixer or food processor fitted with steel blade. Process until well mixed. Add remaining ingredients processing until mixture forms stiff dough.

Shape dough into four logs, each about 1 ¼ inches in diameter. Wrap in plastic wrap or waxed paper and refrigerate for 1 hour or place in freezer for at least 20 minutes. Slice logs into ¼-inch rounds and place on ungreased baking sheets. Bake 12 to 15 minutes until crisp but not browned.

Remove to wire rack to cool. Serve at once or store in airtight container for up to one week.

ROASTED NUT CHICKEN PÁTÉ

YIELD: *2 cups*

Steve Nelson
Waleska, Georgia

4	boneless skinless chicken breast halves (about 1.5 pounds)
½	cup water
¼	cup cream sherry
1	cup broken Georgia pecans
1	cup slivered almonds
¾	cup heavy cream
4	tablespoons cream sherry
4	tablespoons mayonnaise
4	green onions, chopped
1	teaspoon dried thyme
1	teaspoon dried basil
¼	teaspoon salt
½	teaspoon ground black pepper
⅛	teaspoon red pepper
	Fresh basil leaves, optional
	Sweet red pepper, finely diced, optional
	Crackers, toasted pita or bagel slices

Place chicken, water and ¼ cup cream sherry in medium saucepan. Cook, covered, over medium heat about 20 minutes. Drain and set aside to cool. Chop when cool.

Preheat oven to 400°.

Place pecans and almonds on cookie sheet and bake for 10 minutes or until lightly toasted. Stir once while cooking.

Combine heavy cream, 4 tablespoons cream sherry, mayonnaise, green onions, thyme, basil, salt, black pepper and red pepper in food processor. Add chopped chicken and all but 2 tablespoons nuts. Process to form creamy mixture.

Press into bowl. Garnish with reserved 2 tablespoons nuts, fresh basil and diced red pepper.

Chill up to 2 days or serve immediately with crackers, toasted pita or bagel slices.

SAUSAGE CHEESE DIP

YIELD: *4 cups*

2	pounds sausage
2	2-pound boxes processed cheese food
3	10-ounce cans mild tomatoes and green chiles
	Tortilla chips

Brown sausage; break apart and drain well. Melt cheese in microwave, one block at a time. Stir tomatoes into the melted cheese. Add sausage and mix well.

Place in a slow cooker on low for 1 hour or until ready to serve. Serve warm with tortilla chips.

Add 3 teaspoons ground cinnamon with brown sugar for Spiced Pecans.

SINFULLY DELICIOUS SUGARED PECANS  (PICTURED ON PAGE 42)

Mrs. Evelyn Hadden
Augusta, Georgia

YIELD: *2 1/2 cups*

2	egg whites, beaten very stiff
1/2	teaspoon vanilla extract
1	1-pound box light brown sugar
2 - 2 1/2	cups Georgia pecan halves

Preheat oven to 200°.

Combine egg whites and vanilla in large mixing bowl. Add brown sugar; mix well. Fold in pecan halves. Using a fork, individually remove pecans from mixture and place on a greased baking sheet. Bake for 20 minutes. Turn off oven and leave in oven until cool. Store in airtight container.

SMOKED SALMON PECAN SPREAD

YIELD: *2 1/2 cups*

Georgia Pecan Commission

6	ounces smoked salmon fillet, finely chopped
1/2	cup chopped and toasted Georgia pecans
1/2	cup minced Vidalia onion
1/4	cup minced fresh chives
1	cup reduced-fat mayonnaise
1	tablespoon lemon juice
1 - 2	tablespoons capers
1/2	teaspoon freshly ground pepper
	Assorted crackers or toasted French bread slices

Combine ingredients in a small serving bowl; stir to combine. Cover tightly and refrigerate until serving time. Serve with assorted crackers or toasted French bread slices.

STUFFED MUSHROOMS

YIELD: *16 to 24*

1	pound hot sausage
1	pound fresh mushrooms
1	8-ounce jar processed cheese food

Preheat broiler.

Brown sausage in skillet, stirring until crumbly. Drain, reserving 2 tablespoons drippings.

Remove and chop mushroom stems; reserve caps. Sauté stems in reserved drippings until golden brown. Let cool. Add sausage and cheese; mix well. Spoon into mushroom caps; arrange on baking sheet.

Broil 6 inches from heat source for 5 to 7 minutes or until bubbly and brown.

SUGARED PEANUTS

YIELD: *2 cups*

Georgia Peanut
Commission

1	cup sugar
½	cup water
2	cups raw Georgia peanuts, shelled with skins on

Preheat oven to 300°.

Dissolve sugar in water in saucepan over medium heat. Add peanuts and continue to cook over medium heat, stirring frequently. Cook until peanuts are completely sugar coated and no syrup remains in the pan. Pour onto baking sheet, spreading to separate peanuts. Bake for 30 minutes, stirring at 5-minute intervals.

Of course, these are fabulous as a snack, but you might want to consider holding back a batch of these peanuts until after dinner. They are magnificent sprinkled on top of ice cream.

VIDALIA'S FAVORITE ONION DIP

Yield: *4 cups*

Vidalia Onion
Committee

3	cups chopped Vidalia onion
3	cups shredded Swiss cheese
2½	cups mayonnaise
	Garlic salt to taste
	Corn chips

Preheat oven to 350°.

Combine all ingredients except corn chips and pour into a greased 1½-quart baking dish. Bake for 30 to 45 minutes or until lightly browned. Serve with corn chips.

According to the Vidalia Onion Committee, to preserve Vidalia Onions for a longer period of time, wrap them separately in paper towels and refrigerate. Vidalia Onions can also be successfully stored in the legs of clean, sheer pantyhose with a knot tied between each one. Hang in a cool, dry, well-ventilated place. Keep Vidalia Onions cool and dry at all times.

VIDALIA ONION PIE

YIELD: *6 servings*

1	unbaked 9-inch pie crust
2	medium Vidalia onions, sliced
1	tablespoon oil
2	eggs, lightly beaten
¾	cup milk
	Salt and pepper to taste
1	cup grated Cheddar cheese

Preheat oven to 375°

Sauté onions in oil until tender (not brown). Place onions in piecrust.

Combine eggs, milk and seasonings in a small bowl; mix well. Pour mixture over onions in pie crust. Sprinkle with grated cheese. Bake for 40 to 45 minutes.

Perfect on a brunch buffet, served after a round of golf or re-heated as a midnight snack, this pie is hearty yet delicate.

Donnie Walden
Powder Springs, Georgia

WARM TOMATO TACO DIP

YIELD: *4 cups*

½	pound ground beef
1	14.5-ounce can petite diced tomatoes, drained
½	1-ounce package dry taco seasoning mix
1	cup shredded Cheddar cheese
	Sliced green onion, optional
	Ripe avocado, diced, optional
	Sour cream, optional
	Tortilla chips

Preheat oven to 375°.

Brown ground beef in skillet; drain well. Reserve 2 tablespoons tomatoes for garnish. Add remaining tomatoes and ½ package taco seasoning mix to meat; cook over medium heat 5 minutes. Spoon into ½-quart shallow baking dish. Top with cheese.

Bake for 5 minutes or until cheese is melted.

Garnish with reserved tomatoes, sliced green onions, diced avocado and dollops of sour cream, if desired.

Serve with warm tortilla chips.

What is your favorite warm dip? When was the first time you tried it? Were you a party guest or did you make the dip? Consider listing a few of your favorite warm dips and sharing the recipes here.

WATERMELON SALSA (PICTURED ON PAGE 28)

Runette Bell
Jeffersonville, Georgia

YIELD: *4 cups*

4	cups chopped and seeded Georgia watermelon
2	tablespoons lime juice
1	tablespoon finely chopped red onion
1	tablespoon minced fresh cilantro
2	teaspoons finely chopped jalapeño pepper
1/8	teaspoon salt

In a large glass bowl, combine all ingredients. Cover and refrigerate at least one hour or overnight. Serve with a slotted spoon. Excellent over grilled chicken or fish.

ZUCCHINI SQUARES

Bessie Simmons
Cordele, Georgia

YIELD: *24 appetizer servings*

This could also be used as a main dish for lunch with the addition of a fruit salad. If the zucchini is shredded rather than sliced, the squares will cut better.

3	cups thinly sliced zucchini
1/4	teaspoon salt
1/2	cup cooking oil
4	eggs, lightly beaten
1/2	cup finely chopped onion
1	clove garlic, minced
1	cup dry biscuit baking mix
1/2	teaspoon dried oregano
1/2	teaspoon seasoned salt
1/2	cup Parmesan cheese
1	teaspoon dried parsley flakes

Preheat oven to 350°.

Sprinkle salt over zucchini and let stand 20 minutes. Drain well; blot with paper towel.

Combine oil and eggs in a large mixing bowl. Stir in remaining ingredients. Pour into a greased 13x9-inch baking dish. Bake for 30 minutes. Cut into squares to serve.

BREADS

More Georgians will look to their backyards to find ideal ingredients to bake in breads, biscuits and muffins found in this recipe section of Breads. Blackberries are the stars in Berry Patch Bread *(pg. 66)*, while blueberries shine in Blueberry Muffins *(pg. 67)*. Delightful for brunch or with afternoon coffee, Peach Bread *(pg. 71)* is not to be forgotten.

If you haven't tried them, count on Sweet Potato Biscuits *(pg. 74)* becoming new favorites to serve. Golden Hush Puppies *(pg. 70)* will always bring smiles and requests for seconds. Fill your kitchen with the memory-invoking aromas of Basic Buttermilk Biscuits *(pg. 65)* and don't be shy about trying Broccoli Cornbread *(pg. 68)*.

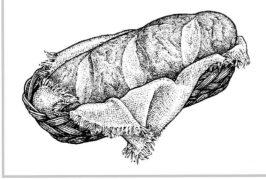

APPLE-DATE LOAF

YIELD: *1 loaf*

1	17-ounce package date quick bread mix
1/2	cup milk
1/2	cup sour cream
1	cup peeled and finely chopped Georgia apple
1	egg
1/2	teaspoon apple pie spice

Preheat oven to 350°.

Combine all ingredients in a large mixing bowl; stir just until dry ingredients are moistened. Spoon batter into greased and floured 8 1/2x4 1/2-inch loaf pan.

Bake for 1 hour and 10 minutes or until pick inserted in center comes out clean. Cool in pan on wire rack 10 minutes; remove from pan and cool on wire rack.

BANANA BREAD

YIELD: *1 loaf*

Marcia Headden
Atlanta, Georgia

2	cups all-purpose flour
1	teaspoon baking soda
1/2	teaspoon salt
1/2	cup butter
1	cup sugar
2	eggs
1	cup mashed ripe banana
1/3	cup milk
1	teaspoon lemon juice
1/2	cup chopped Georgia pecans

Preheat oven to 350°.

Sift together flour, soda and salt. Cream butter and sugar in large bowl of electric mixer; add eggs and bananas, mixing well. Combine milk and lemon juice; fold into creamed mixture alternately with flour mixture. Stir in pecans. Pour into greased and floured 9x5-inch loaf pan.

Bake for 1 hour or until wooden pick inserted in center comes out clean.

Cool in pan on wire rack for 10 minutes; remove from pan and cool on wire rack.

BASIC BUTTERMILK BISCUITS   (PICTURED ON PAGE 36)

YIELD: *12 biscuits*

2	cups self-rising flour
1	teaspoon sugar
1/3	cup shortening, butter or margarine
3/4	cup buttermilk
	Melted butter or margarine

Preheat oven to 450°.

Combine flour and sugar in large bowl; mix well. Cut in shortening with pastry blender until mixture resembles coarse crumbs. Add buttermilk; stir with fork until soft dough forms and mixture begins to pull away from sides of bowl.

Knead dough on lightly floured surface, just until smooth. Roll out dough to 1/2-inch thickness. Cut with floured 2 1/2-inch round cutter. Place on ungreased cookie sheet.

Bake for 12 to 14 minutes or until golden brown. Brush with melted butter. Serve warm.

To substitute for buttermilk, use 2 teaspoons vinegar or lemon juice plus enough milk to make 3/4 cup.

Spoon Berry Patch Bread batter into greased miniature muffin pans and bake at 400° for 15 to 20 minutes. Yield: 4 dozen miniature muffins.

BERRY PATCH BREAD

YIELD: *1 13x9-inch bread*

1	8-ounce package cream cheese
1	cup sugar
½	cup butter or margarine
2	eggs
2	cups sifted cake flour
1	teaspoon baking powder
½	teaspoon baking soda
¼	teaspoon salt
¼	cup milk
½	teaspoon vanilla extract
1	cup fresh blackberries
¼	cup blackberry jam
½	cup chopped Georgia pecans

Preheat oven to 350°.

Combine cream cheese, sugar and butter in a large mixer bowl. Beat with mixer until well blended. Add eggs, beating well after each. Sift dry ingredients; add alternately with milk, mixing well after each addition. Stir in vanilla, blackberries and jam.

Pour into greased and floured 13x9-inch baking pan.

Bake for 35 minutes.

BLUEBERRY MUFFINS

Angie McGinnis
Danielsville, Georgia

YIELD: *18 muffins*

2	cups all-purpose flour
2/3	cup sugar
1	tablespoon baking powder
1/2	teaspoon salt
1/2	teaspoon nutmeg
1 1/2	cups fresh Georgia blueberries
2	eggs, beaten
1/2	cup milk
1/2	cup butter, melted
1/4	cup chopped Georgia pecans
2	tablespoons sugar

Preheat oven to 400°.

Combine flour, 2/3 cup sugar, baking powder, salt and nutmeg in a large mixing bowl. Toss in blueberries to coat. Stir together eggs, butter and milk in a small bowl. Add liquid ingredients to dry ingredients, stirring just to moisten. Fill greased muffin pans two-thirds full. Sprinkle tops with pecans and sugar.

Bake for 15 to 20 minutes.

BROCCOLI CORNBREAD

YIELD: *8 to 10 servings*

1	10-ounce package frozen chopped broccoli, thawed and drained
¾	cup cottage cheese
1	large onion, chopped
4	eggs, beaten
½	cup melted butter or margarine
1	8-ounce package cornbread mix

Preheat oven to 425˚.

Combine first 5 ingredients in a large bowl; mix until well blended. Add cornbread mix, stirring just until moistened.

Spoon batter into a greased 10-inch iron skillet or 9-inch square baking pan.

Bake for 30 to 35 minutes.

BUTTERMILK PANCAKES

YIELD: *16 pancakes*

2	eggs
2	cups buttermilk
¼	cup vegetable oil
1¾	cups self-rising flour
2	tablespoons sugar
½	teaspoon baking soda
½	teaspoon salt

Griddle is ready when small drops of water sizzle and disappear almost immediately. Pancakes will stick if griddle is too cool.

Heat griddle or large skillet to medium high. Grease lightly with oil.

Beat eggs in a large bowl. Add buttermilk and oil; mix well. Add remaining ingredients; stir just until large lumps disappear. For thicker pancakes, add additional flour; for thinner pancakes, add additional buttermilk.

Pour about ¼ cup batter onto hot griddle for each pancake. Cook 1 to 2 minutes or until bubbles begin to break on surface. Turn; cook 1 to 2 minutes or until golden brown.

CHEWY BRAN MUFFINS

YIELD: *24 muffins*

Mary Behling
Shady Dale, Georgia

2½	cups bran flakes cereal
1½	cup milk
½	cup vegetable oil
2	eggs, beaten
1	8-ounce can crushed pineapple in juice, undrained
1½	cups all-purpose flour
3	teaspoons baking powder
½	teaspoon salt
½	cup sugar
1	cup finely chopped Georgia pecans
1	cup flaked coconut

Preheat oven to 400°

Combine bran flakes and milk in a large mixing bowl. Set aside to allow cereal to soften. When softened, stir in oil, eggs and pineapple.

Sift flour, baking powder, salt and sugar. Stir into cereal mixture. Add pecans and coconut, mixing well. Spoon mixture into greased and floured or paper lined muffin pans.

Bake for 25 minutes or until golden brown. Remove from pans to cool.

CRISP WAFFLES

YIELD: *8 large waffles*

2½	cups all-purpose flour
1	tablespoon plus 1 teaspoon baking powder
¾	teaspoon salt
1½	tablespoons sugar
2	eggs, beaten
2½	cups milk
¾	cup vegetable oil

Preheat electric waffle iron. Combine first 4 ingredients in a large mixing bowl. Combine eggs, milk and oil; add to flour mixture, stirring just until dry ingredients are moistened.

Cook in a preheated waffle iron until golden.

GOLDEN HUSH PUPPIES

YIELD: *18 hush puppies*

2	cups self-rising cornmeal
1	teaspoon salt
1	medium onion, finely chopped
¼	cup buttermilk
1	egg, slightly beaten
	Vegetable oil

Combine cornmeal, salt and onion in medium mixing bowl; add buttermilk and egg, stirring only until dry ingredients are wet. Carefully drop batter by tablespoon into deep hot oil (370°) and fry 2 to 3 minutes, turning once. Drain on absorbent paper.

OVERNIGHT PECAN FRENCH TOAST

Georgia Pecan Commission

YIELD: *4 servings*

8	1-inch thick slices French bread
4	eggs, lightly beaten
⅔	cup orange juice
⅓	cup milk
¼	cup sugar
¼	teaspoon ground nutmeg
½	teaspoon vanilla extract
⅓	cup butter, melted
½	cup chopped Georgia pecans
	Syrup and butter, optional

Place bread slices in lightly greased 9x13-inch baking dish. Combine eggs, juice, milk, sugar, nutmeg, vanilla and melted butter; stir to mix. Pour milk mixture over bread slices, soaking each slice with mixture. Cover and refrigerate overnight.

Preheat oven to 375°.

Sprinkle bread with pecans. Bake for 25 to 30 minutes or until light brown. Serve with syrup and butter, if desired.

PEACH BREAD

YIELD: *2 loaves*

Georgia Peach
Commission

1 ½	cups sugar
½	cup shortening
2	eggs
2 ¼	cups puréed fresh Georgia peaches (approximately 6 to 8 medium)
2	cups all-purpose flour
1	teaspoon ground cinnamon
1	teaspoon baking soda
1	teaspoon baking powder
¼	teaspoon salt
1	teaspoon vanilla extract
1	cup finely chopped Georgia pecans

Preheat oven to 325°.

Cream sugar and shortening in large bowl of electric mixer. Add eggs and mix well. Add peach purée and dry ingredients. Stir to combine. Fold in vanilla and pecans. Pour into 2 greased and floured 9x5-inch loaf pans.

Bake for 55 to 60 minutes. Remove from oven and cool 10 minutes on wire rack. Remove bread from pan and cool before slicing.

Last minute overnight guests? Keep a loaf of this Peach Bread in your freezer and breakfast will be a breeze when you serve it with morning coffee. Being prepared is a Southerner's method of stress management.

QUICK BLUEBERRY MUFFINS

YIELD: *12 muffins*

Velma Elzey
Cumming, Georgia

1	egg, beaten
2	tablespoons vegetable oil
$2/3$	cup milk
2	cups dry biscuit baking mix
$1/3$	cup sugar
$3/4$ - 1	cup fresh Georgia blueberries

Preheat oven to 400°.

Grease bottoms only of 12-cup muffin pan. Set aside.

Combine egg, oil and milk in a large mixing bowl; stir to combine. Add baking mix and sugar. Stir only until dry ingredients are moistened. Fold in blueberries; spoon mixture into muffin pans.

Bake for 15 to 18 minutes.

RAISIN BRAN REFRIGERATOR MUFFINS

YIELD: *4 dozen muffins*

Hilda Dortch
Smyrna, Georgia

The batter can be refrigerated for 3 weeks. Muffins also freeze well after baking.

1	15-ounce box raisin bran cereal
1	quart buttermilk
1	cup vegetable oil
3	cups sugar
2	teaspoons salt
3	teaspoons baking soda
5	cups all-purpose flour
2	teaspoons vanilla extract
4	eggs, beaten

Preheat oven to 350°.

Combine cereal and buttermilk in a large mixing bowl. Let stand for 5 minutes.

Combine dry ingredients. Set aside.

Combine cereal mixture, oil and dry ingredients; mix until combined. Mixture will be very thick. Add eggs and vanilla. Stir well. Spoon into greased muffin pans.

Bake for 15 to 20 minutes.

SOUTHERN STYLE BUTTERMILK CORNBREAD (PICTURED ON PAGE 44)

YIELD: *10 servings*

4	cups cornmeal
2	teaspoons salt
2	teaspoons baking soda
4	eggs, beaten
4	cups buttermilk
$\frac{1}{2}$	cup bacon drippings or vegetable oil

Preheat oven to 400°. Place a well-greased $10\frac{1}{2}$-inch cast iron skillet in oven while preheating until skillet is very hot.

Combine dry ingredients in large mixing bowl; add eggs and buttermilk, mixing well. Stir in bacon drippings.

Pour batter into hot skillet. Bake for 40 minutes or until golden brown.

SPOON ROLLS

Maurine Fox
Powder Springs, Georgia

YIELD: *12 rolls*

2	cups self-rising flour
$\frac{1}{4}$	cup sugar
$\frac{1}{4}$	cup melted shortening
$\frac{3}{4}$	cup warm water
1	package dry yeast

Preheat oven to 400°.

Combine all ingredients in large mixing bowl. Mix well; drop by tablespoons into well-greased muffin pans.

Bake for 15 minutes.

Serve with dinner and, if there are any leftovers, you may want to devour them with breakfast. Slightly re-heat the biscuits and spread them with Georgia honey.

SWEET POTATO BISCUITS

YIELD: *18 biscuits*

2	cups self-rising flour
1/3	cup sugar
3	tablespoons shortening
2	tablespoons butter or margarine
1	cup cooked mashed sweet potato
1/3	cup milk or half-and-half

Preheat oven to 400°.

Combine flour and sugar in a medium bowl; cut in shortening and butter with a pastry blender until mixture is crumbly. Add mashed sweet potato and milk, stirring just until dry ingredients are moistened. Turn dough onto floured surface, and knead 4 or 5 times.

Roll dough to 1/2-inch thickness; cut with a 2-inch biscuit cutter. Place on lightly greased baking sheet.

Bake for 12 to 15 minutes or until light golden brown.

SALADS

Using many Georgia-grown ingredients — from a patch of Georgia blackberries to a field of green beans — this section will inspire you to try new tastes and textures.

The Blackberry Congealed Salad *(pg. 78)* was created by a thoughtful grandmother wanting to please her granddaughter. Crunchy Green Bean Salad *(pg. 80)* is an excellent make-ahead dish well-suited for entertaining. Once you start preparing Onion and Steak Salad *(pg. 83)* you'll discover most men find it irresistible — even those who claim not to like salad. What's not to like?

Pink Cloud Frozen Salad *(pg. 84)* signals "celebration" and through the years has been a colorful and tasty addition to many baby showers and luncheons. Whether you are packing Festive Pasta Salad *(pg. 81)* for a picnic in the park or serving Seafood Louis Salad *(pg. 85)*, when it's your turn to host the girls for lunch, turning to these recipes will bring years of delicious rewards.

Pull out your fancy stemmed glasses for individual servings of this Southern classic.

AMBROSIA SALAD

YIELD: *6 to 8 servings*

9	oranges, peeled, seeded and sectioned
2	20-ounce cans crushed pineapple, drained
½	cup sugar, if desired
1	cup flaked coconut

Combine all ingredients in a large bowl, cover and refrigerate overnight.

APPLE CHICKEN SALAD

YIELD: *6 servings*

Georgia Apple Commission

3	cups unpeeled and diced sweet red Georgia apples
2	cups cooked and diced chicken breast
1	cup thinly sliced celery
½	cup raisins
½	cup chopped and toasted Georgia pecans
½	cup sour cream
½	cup mayonnaise
1	tablespoon lemon juice
2	tablespoons sugar

Combine apples, chicken, celery, raisins and pecans in large serving bowl. Combine remaining ingredients in a small mixing bowl; stir to combine. Pour dressing over salad; toss to coat. Cover and refrigerate until ready to serve.

APPLE SLAW

YIELD: *6 servings*

Marjorie Brownlea
Valdosta, Georgia

3	tablespoons olive oil
2	tablespoons mayonnaise
1	tablespoon mustard
1	tablespoon lemon juice
¼	teaspoon hot sauce
1	16-ounce package shredded slaw mix with carrots and red cabbage
1	large Georgia apple, peeled and finely chopped
	Salt and black pepper to taste

Combine oil, mayonnaise, mustard, lemon juice and hot sauce in a large bowl. Stir to combine. Add slaw mix and apple, tossing well to coat. Add salt and pepper to taste. Chill before serving.

Cooked, crumbled bacon makes a nice addition to this recipe. Use a tart apple for a more intense taste.

From late August to December, roadside stands and retailers offer tree-ripened apples from Ellijay, Georgia, the apple capital of the state, to the mountains of North Georgia. Among the varieties are: Granny Smith, Golden Delicious, Red Delicious, Gold Rush, Detroit, Jonathan, Empire, Swiss Gourmet, Ozark Gold, Pink Lady, Winesap, Arkansas Black, and many others.

Juanita Williams
Kennesaw, Georgia

BLACKBERRY CONGEALED SALAD

YIELD: *6 servings*

2	cups fresh blackberries
3/4	cup sugar
1	3-ounce package blackberry flavor gelatin
1 1/2	cups boiling water
3/4	cup mayonnaise
3/4	cup cottage cheese
3/4	cup French vanilla flavor frozen whipped topping, thawed
3/4	cup chopped Georgia pecans

Rinse and drain blackberries. Combine blackberries and sugar in a small bowl. Set aside.

Combine gelatin and boiling water in a large bowl; stir until completely dissolved. Refrigerate until slightly set (about the consistency of egg whites).

Combine mayonnaise, cottage cheese and whipped topping in a small mixing bowl. Beat until well blended and creamy. Fold into gelatin. Stir in blackberries and sugar. Stir until ingredients are blended. Stir in pecans.

Pour into a 1-quart container and refrigerate until set.

"This recipe is the result of my granddaughter wanting to pick blackberries and use them in gelatin. It was a big hit with the family."

— Juanita Williams

Frozen blackberries can be used if fresh are unavailable, however, they will have more liquid after thawing. Adding 1 envelope unflavored gelatin dissolved in 1/4 cup cold water will help congeal the salad if frozen fruit is used.

Fresh or frozen blueberries can be substituted for blackberries.

CHUNKY VEGETABLE SALAD

YIELD: *6 to 8 servings*

2	cups peeled and chopped cucumber
1	cup chopped red bell pepper
1	cup chopped yellow bell pepper
1	cup chopped green pepper
1	cup chopped tomato
1/2	cup chopped Vidalia onion
1	tablespoon fresh lemon juice
1	teaspoon olive oil
1/2	teaspoon salt
1/4	teaspoon Dijon mustard
1/8	teaspoon pepper
2	cloves garlic, minced
	Leaf lettuce, optional

Combine vegetables in a large glass bowl. Combine remaining ingredients except lettuce in small bowl; stir well to combine. Pour dressing over vegetables; toss gently to coat. Serve over lettuce leaves.

COPPER PENNIES

YIELD: *6 to 8 servings*

Claudia Cason
Tifton, Georgia

This salad keeps well in the refrigerator for a week or more.

2	pounds carrots, peeled and sliced
1	medium size onion, chopped
1	medium size green pepper, chopped
1	$10^{3/4}$-ounce can tomato soup
1/4	cup vegetable oil
1/4	cup vinegar
3/4	cup sugar
1	teaspoon mustard
1	teaspoon Worcestershire sauce
	Dash hot sauce
	Salt and pepper to taste

Combine carrots, onion and green pepper in a large glass bowl. Set aside.

Combine remaining ingredients in a small bowl, mix well and pour over vegetables. Cover tightly and refrigerate overnight.

CRANBERRY SALAD

Mary Barnette
Cartersville, Georgia

YIELD: *12 servings*

1	12-ounce package fresh cranberries
½	cup water
1 ½	cups sugar
1	20-ounce can crushed pineapple with juice, undrained
1	cup mayonnaise
1	cup chopped Georgia pecans
2	3-ounce packages cherry gelatin
3	cups boiling water

Combine cranberries, water and sugar in large saucepan. Cook over medium heat until berries pop. Remove from heat, mash well. Add remaining ingredients. Mix well. Pour mixture into a 9-x13-inch pan or 4 quart mold. Refrigerate until set.

CRUNCHY GREEN BEAN SALAD

Jean Perkins
Valdosta, Georgia

YIELD: *6 servings*

1	pound fresh green beans, trimmed
2	tablespoons water
2	cups halved cherry or grape tomatoes
1	medium Vidalia onion, thinly sliced
3	tablespoons extra virgin olive oil
3	tablespoons red wine vinegar
2	tablespoons balsamic vinegar
½	teaspoon sugar
1	tablespoon chopped fresh basil

Place green beans and water in a microwave safe bowl; cover tightly and microwave on HIGH for 5 minutes. Drain, rinse with cold water and chill quickly.

Combine beans, tomatoes and onions in large glass bowl. Set aside.

Combine oil, vinegars, sugar and basil in a small bowl. Whisk until well combined.

Pour over vegetable mixture; refrigerate several hours to allow flavors to blend.

To lighten the salad, omit mayonnaise.

The grated rind of 1 orange will complement the cranberry flavor.

The salad does not set up to be extremely firm due to the high sugar content. If a firmer salad is desired, dissolve 1 envelope unflavored gelatin in ¼ cup cold water and add to the mixture.

Beans can be cooked in boiling water in large saucepan for 3 to 5 minutes, drained and chilled.

White or cider vinegar can be substituted for red wine and balsamic.

This salad probably brings back memories of grandma or grandpa stringing and snapping green beans on the back porch.

DEVILISH EGGS

YIELD: *8 servings*

Georgia Egg
Commission

8	hard-cooked eggs
¼	cup mayonnaise
1	teaspoon prepared mustard
½ - 1	teaspoon prepared horseradish
¼	teaspoon salt
¼	teaspoon pepper
	Paprika

Cut eggs in half lengthwise; remove yolks. Mash yolks; stir in mayonnaise, mustard, horseradish, salt and pepper. Fill egg halves with mixture; chill. Sprinkle with paprika before serving.

FESTIVE PASTA SALAD

YIELD: *12 servings*

Joanna Patterson
Duluth, Georgia

1	16-ounce package elbow macaroni or rotini pasta, cooked and cooled
4	cups fresh vegetables of your choice — sliced celery, chopped red or green peppers, sliced radishes, chopped Vidalia onions, shredded carrots, tiny broccoli florets, or peeled and shredded broccoli stems
¼	cup chopped flat leaf parsley
1 ¼	cup low fat mayonnaise
1	8-ounce container plain yogurt
¼	cup cider vinegar
1	tablespoon Dijon mustard
1	tablespoon sugar
1	teaspoon salt
½	teaspoon ground black pepper

Combine cooked, cooled pasta and vegetables in a large bowl. In a medium bowl, combine remaining ingredients for dressing. Pour over pasta and vegetables; stir gently to combine. Refrigerate several hours or overnight.

"This makes a large amount of salad, but it keeps well. It's great in a brown bag lunch or for a cool, refreshing lunch at home when you've been working in the garden all morning in the hot Georgia sunshine."
— *Joanna Patterson*

Check the yogurt label — if it contains sugar, omit the sugar in the dressing.

This is a really rich salad; it could easily double as a dessert.

GRAPE SALAD

YIELD: *8 to 10 servings*

Jo Anne Coleman
Conyers, Georgia

1 ½	pounds seedless red grapes
1	8-ounce carton sour cream
1	8-ounce package cream cheese, softened
½	cup sugar
¼	cup firmly packed light brown sugar
½	cup chopped Georgia pecans

Wash grapes and dry thoroughly. Set aside.

Combine sour cream, cream cheese and granulated sugar in medium mixing bowl. Mix until smooth and well blended. Place half of grapes in glass serving bowl. Pour half cream cheese mixture over grapes; smooth with spoon. Sprinkle half of brown sugar and half of pecans over mixture. Repeat layers.

Cover and refrigerate.

LAYERED VEGETABLE SALAD

YIELD: *10 to 12 servings*

4	cups torn lettuce
1	cup chopped celery
1	cup chopped green pepper
1	cup chopped Vidalia onion
1	10-ounce package frozen English peas, thawed
3	cups fresh spinach, torn
3	cups chopped smoked turkey, optional
¾	cup mayonnaise
¾	cup sour cream
½	cup finely shredded Cheddar cheese
6	slices bacon, cooked and crumbled

Layer first 7 ingredients in large glass serving bowl.

Combine mayonnaise and sour cream in a small bowl, stirring well. Spread over salad, sealing to edges of bowl. Sprinkle cheese and bacon in center before serving.

MARINATED VEGETABLE SALAD

YIELD: *8 to 10 servings*

Letha Hayes
Hazlehurst, Georgia

1	15-ounce can green peas, drained
1	11-ounce can whole kernel corn, drained
1	14-ounce can French style green beans, drained
1	2-ounce jar chopped pimento, drained
1	cup chopped celery
½	cup chopped green pepper
½	cup chopped onion
¾	cup vinegar
1	cup sugar
½	cup vegetable oil
1	teaspoon salt
1	teaspoon pepper

Combine vegetables in a large glass bowl. Set aside.

Combine vinegar and sugar in small saucepan. Bring to a boil, remove from heat and add oil. Pour mixture over vegetables. Add salt and pepper.

Cover and refrigerate.

This recipe is best when made ahead and refrigerated to let the flavors blend.

Any combination of canned vegetables can be used in this recipe.

For a lighter salad, use ¼ cup oil, ½ cup vinegar and ¼ cup sugar.

ONION AND STEAK SALAD

YIELD: *4 servings*

Vidalia Onion Committee

2	tablespoons chopped fresh parsley
1	tablespoon olive oil
1	tablespoon water
1	tablespoon red wine vinegar
1	clove garlic, minced
1	medium Vidalia onion, thinly sliced
¾	pound lean broiled steak, cut into 1-inch strips
¾	cup sliced radishes
	Leaf lettuce
1	cup crumbled blue cheese

Combine parsley, oil, water, vinegar and garlic in a small bowl, stirring to mix well.

Set aside. Lightly toss remaining ingredients except blue cheese in a large salad bowl. Pour dressing over salad and toss. Sprinkle with blue cheese. Serve immediately.

PINK CLOUD FROZEN SALAD

Georgia Milk Commission

YIELD: *9 servings*

1	8-ounce package cream cheese, softened
¼	cup honey
1	10-ounce package frozen strawberries, partially thawed
2	bananas, sliced
2	cups miniature marshmallows
1	cup whipping cream, whipped

Beat cream cheese in large bowl until smooth. Add honey and continue beating until well blended. Stir in strawberries, bananas and marshmallows. Gently fold in whipped cream.

Pour into 9-inch square baking pan. Cover with foil and freeze until firm. To serve, let stand at room temperature 20 minutes. Cut into squares.

Spoon salad into paper-lined muffin tins for individual salads. Cover and freeze. Before serving, remove paper liners.

RICH'S MAGNOLIA ROOM CHICKEN SALAD AMANDINE

Louise Barbee
Lithia Springs, Georgia

YIELD: *4 cups*

3½	pounds chicken breasts with ribs
1	teaspoon salt
6	stalks celery, diced
½	cup sweet pickle relish
1½	teaspoons white pepper
2	cups mayonnaise
½	cup sliced almonds or Georgia pecans, toasted

Place chicken breasts in Dutch oven; add water to cover and salt. Bring to a boil over medium heat. Reduce heat and simmer until chicken is tender, approximately 45 minutes. Let chicken cool and remove meat from bones. Cut into medium size strips.

Combine celery, pickle relish, pepper and mayonnaise in a large bowl. Add chicken and mix well. Cover and refrigerate until ready to serve. Garnish with almonds or pecans.

3 cups chopped, cooked chicken can be substituted for the chicken breasts.

Rich's Department Store in downtown Atlanta was "the place" for white gloves and ladies' lunches in the 1950s. The Magnolia Room served this famous Chicken Salad Amandine.

SEAFOOD LOUIS SALAD

YIELD: *8 servings*

1	cup mayonnaise
¼	cup chili sauce
3	green onions, chopped
1	teaspoon lemon juice
¼	teaspoon salt
3	tablespoons whipping cream
1	head iceberg lettuce, shredded
1	pound fresh crabmeat, drained and flaked
1	pound peeled, cooked Georgia shrimp
2	large tomatoes, cut into thin wedges
4	hard-cooked eggs, cut into wedges

Combine first 6 ingredients in a large bowl, whisking until well blended; set aside.

Place shredded lettuce on a platter; arrange crabmeat, shrimp, tomato wedges and egg wedges on lettuce. Serve with dressing on the side.

SOUR CREAM POTATO SALAD

YIELD: *8 servings*

5	pounds medium red potatoes
1	cup mayonnaise
1	8-ounce carton sour cream
2	teaspoons prepared horseradish
1½	teaspoons celery seed
1	teaspoon salt
1	medium onion, chopped
1	cup chopped parsley
1	teaspoon dried dill weed

Scrub potatoes; boil until fork tender. Drain, cool, peel and cut into cubes.

Mix mayonnaise, sour cream, horseradish and celery seed in small bowl. Stir in onion, parsley and dill weed.

Combine potatoes and dressing in large bowl, stirring only until potatoes are well coated with dressing. Cover and chill.

When boiling potatoes for potato salad, always start by placing potatoes in a pot of cold water. This will prevent the potatoes from becoming overcooked and mushy on the outside and undercooked and hard on the inside.

Strawberry Spinach Salad with Sugared Pecans and Poppy Seed Dressing

Bebe Frazier
St. Simons, Georgia

YIELD: *8 servings*

Strawberry Spinach Salad

1	10-ounce bag fresh spinach
1	pint strawberries, sliced
	Poppy Seed Dressing
	Sugared Pecans

Combine spinach and strawberries in a large bowl. Toss to combine. Add enough Poppy Seed Dressing to coat spinach. Place on individual serving plates. Top with Sugared Pecans.

Poppy Seed Dressing

⅓	cup white vinegar
⅓	cup sugar
1	teaspoon dry mustard
½	teaspoon salt
¾	cup vegetable oil
1	small red onion, chopped
1	tablespoon poppy seeds

Combine vinegar, sugar, mustard and salt in a small mixing bowl. Stir until sugar dissolves. Add oil, whisking until it is incorporated into the mixture. Stir in onion and poppy seeds. Refrigerate at least 1 hour before serving.

Sugared Pecans

| 1 | cup toasted and coarsely chopped Georgia pecans |
| 3 | tablespoons sugar |

Place sugar in heavy bottom skillet. Heat over medium-high heat until sugar melts. Remove from heat and stir in pecans to coat. Pour onto buttered foil to cool. Break into small pieces when cool.

SUMMER FRUIT SALAD WITH PEACHY DRESSING

Georgia Peach
Commission

YIELD: *10 to 12 servings*

½	cantaloupe, seeded, peeled and chopped
½	honeydew melon, seeded, peeled and chopped
3	cups seeded and chopped Georgia watermelon
1	cup strawberries
1	cup sliced Georgia peaches
1	cup Georgia apple chunks
1	cup Georgia blueberries
2	kiwi, peeled and sliced
	Peachy Dressing

Combine ingredients in large serving bowl. Prepare Peachy Dressing.

At serving time, pour dressing over fruit and toss lightly to coat fruit.

Peachy Dressing

YIELD: *1 ½ cups*

2	Georgia peaches, peeled, seeded and diced
½	cup sour cream or plain low-fat yogurt
2	tablespoons firmly packed light brown sugar
1 ½	teaspoons lemon juice

Combine all ingredients in blender or food processor. Process until smooth; pour into 2-cup container; cover, and refrigerate until ready to serve. At serving time pour over Summer Fruit Salad and toss lightly.

SOUPS/STEWS/CHILI

Travel to different regions of our state and beyond with this section's assortment of soups, stews and chili.

For a culinary visit to the Big Easy, try Chili Creole *(pg. 93)* jazzed with all the right seasonings. Two versions of Brunswick Stew *(pg. 91 & pg. 95)* will satisfy both busy cooks and traditionalists. Vegetable gardeners will want to try and share Summer Garden Minestrone *(pg. 101)*. Consider Baked Potato Soup *(pg. 89)* if you are searching for something hearty to serve during halftime. Or, if an outdoor concert event is calling for you to pack something chilled, turn to Cold Vegetable Soup *(pg. 94)* for zest and flavor. These inspiring recipes will offer you comfort inside and out.

BAKED POTATO SOUP

YIELD: *10 cups*

Betty Hensley
Old Fort, North Carolina

4	large baking potatoes
2/3	cup butter or margarine
2/3	cup all-purpose flour
6	cups milk
3/4	teaspoon salt
1/2	teaspoon pepper
1 1/2	cups (6 ounces) shredded Cheddar cheese, divided
12	slices bacon, cooked and crumbled, divided
4	green onions, sliced, divided
1	8-ounce carton sour cream

Preheat oven to 400°.

Wash potatoes; pierce several times with a fork. Bake for 45 minutes or until tender. Cut potatoes in half lengthwise; scoop out pulp, and reserve. Discard shells.

Melt butter in a Dutch oven over low heat; add flour stirring until smooth. Cook 1 minute, stirring constantly. Gradually add milk; cook over medium heat, stirring constantly, until thickened and bubbly.

Stir in potato, salt, pepper, 1 cup cheese, 1/2 cup bacon, 2 tablespoons green onions and sour cream; cook just until heated (do not boil). Ladle into serving bowls and sprinkle with remaining cheese, bacon, and green onions.

Try establishing soup night in your home, and amaze your family with a wide variety of soups. Add a salad and a light dessert and encourage family members to take turns in the kitchen creating and preparing soup night.

Eliminating the blender step will result in a "chunkier" soup. This is a good way to use leftover broccoli.

BROCCOLI CHEESE SOUP

YIELD: *4 to 6 servings*

Shirley Cobb
Franklin, Georgia

1	10-ounce package frozen broccoli
1	medium onion, chopped
3	tablespoons butter or margarine
1/4	cup chopped fresh parsley, optional
2	cups chicken broth, divided
2	cups half-and-half or milk
3/4	teaspoon salt
1/4	teaspoon garlic powder
1/2	teaspoon lemon-pepper seasoning
1/8	teaspoon red pepper
1/4	cup all-purpose flour
2	cups shredded sharp Cheddar cheese
	Additional chopped parsley

Cook broccoli according to package directions; drain well, set aside.

Sauté onion in butter in a large saucepan until tender; add reserved broccoli and 1/4 cup parsley, if desired, and cook 3 minutes, stirring constantly.

Transfer broccoli mixture to container of an electric blender; add 1 cup chicken broth and process until smooth.

Return mixture to saucepan; add remaining broth, half-and-half, salt, garlic powder, lemon-pepper seasoning, pepper and flour, stirring well. Stir in cheese. Cook over medium heat 5 minutes or until thoroughly heated. Ladle into individual serving bowls; garnish with additional chopped parsley. Serve warm.

Brunswick Stew

YIELD: *approximately 15 cups*

Dianne Davis
Douglasville, Georgia

1	pound pork (bone-in)
1	pound chicken (bone-in)
1	pound beef chuck roast (bone-in)
10	cups water
4	cups finely chopped onion
4	cups finely chopped celery
5	tablespoons Worcestershire sauce
2	jalapeño peppers, whole
4	14.5-ounce cans diced tomatoes
1	40-ounce bottle ketchup
2	15-ounce cans whole kernel corn, drained
	Salt and pepper to taste

Combine pork, chicken, beef and 10 cups water in large stockpot. Bring to a boil, reduce heat and simmer several hours, until meat falls off the bone. Remove meat from broth; reserve broth.

Remove bones and fat from meat and discard. Place meat in large container of food processor; process until mixture is finely chopped. Return to broth; add remaining ingredients except corn.

Bring to a boil, reduce heat and simmer for 1 1/2 hours. Add corn and cook an additional 15 minutes.

Janice Stone
Jasper, Georgia

CHICKEN TORTELLINI SOUP

YIELD: *12 servings*

4	cups water
4	10½-ounce cans condensed chicken broth
3	boneless, skinless chicken breasts, cooked (about 4 cups cooked chicken)
2	10½-ounce cans cream of chicken soup
1	large onion, chopped
3	cloves garlic, minced
¾	teaspoon dried basil
¾	teaspoon dried oregano
1	16-ounce package frozen cauliflower, broccoli and carrot mixture
1	8-ounce package cheese tortellini
¾	cup grated Parmesan cheese
½	cup diced tomatoes

In a large saucepot, combine water, chicken broth, chicken, cream of chicken soup, onion, garlic, basil and oregano. Cover; bring to a boil. Add vegetables and tortellini; cover, reduce heat and simmer 20 minutes. Ladle into soup bowls. Garnish with cheese and diced tomatoes.

Other flavors of tortellini, which can be found in the refrigerated section of the supermarket, can be used.

If using ready-to-serve broth, omit water and increase broth to 6 (14-ounce) cans.

CHILI CREOLE   (PICTURED ON PAGE 46)

YIELD: *6 to 8 servings*

Ronald C. Treadaway, Sr.
Acworth, Georgia

2	tablespoons shortening
1½ - 2	pounds round steak, cut into bite-size pieces
1	medium onion, chopped
1	medium green pepper, chopped
1	bunch green onions, chopped
5½	cups water
2	tablespoons chili powder
½	teaspoon Creole seasoning
¼	teaspoon dry mustard
¼	teaspoon hot sauce
1	tablespoon instant blending flour
2	tablespoons water
2	6-ounce cans tomato paste
1	16-ounce can New Orleans-style red kidney beans
1	2-ounce jar chopped pimento, optional
2	teaspoons salt
	Pepper to taste

Place shortening and round steak in large Dutch oven or stock pot. Cook over medium heat until steak is browned. Remove steak and set aside.

Add onion, green pepper and green onions to Dutch oven. Cook until tender, about 5 minutes, stirring often. Stir in water, chili powder, Creole seasoning, dry mustard and hot sauce. Cook over medium heat 20 minutes, stirring often.

Combine instant blending flour and 2 tablespoons water. Add to Dutch oven, stirring well. Stir in tomato paste, kidney beans and reserved meat.

Cook over low heat for 45 minutes, or until sauce reaches desired consistency. Add pimento, if desired, during last 10 minutes of cooking. Add salt and pepper to taste.

1½ cups of beer can be substituted for 1½ cups water, if desired.

Nearly every cook has a secret chili recipe, whether it's passed down from family members or concocted after much testing. Do you have a favorite recipe for chili? Use this page to mention different occasions when you served the chili and explain the origin of your recipe.

CHILI GRANDE

Kelley Turk
Conyers, Georgia

YIELD: *8 cups*

1	pound lean stew beef, cut into 3/4-inch cubes
1	teaspoon chili powder
1	teaspoon garlic salt
1/2	teaspoon cumin powder
2	15 1/2-ounce cans spicy chili beans, undrained
1	14 1/2-ounce can diced tomatoes, undrained
1	4 1/2-ounce can chopped green chilies
1	10-ounce package frozen chopped green pepper
1	small onion, chopped

Combine all ingredients in a slow cooker; stir well. Cover and cook on HIGH for 4 hours. Or, cover and cook on HIGH 1 hour, reduce heat to LOW and cook 6 hours.

This is delicious served in easy-to-make tortilla bowls. Place 10-inch flour tortillas in 1½-quart glass bowl. Microwave on HIGH 2 minutes or until crisp. Serve chili in tortilla bowls topped with sour cream.

COLD VEGETABLE SOUP   (PICTURED ON PAGE 21)

YIELD: *7 cups*

2	medium tomatoes, chopped into chunks
1	cup chopped celery,
1/2	cup chopped Vidalia onion
2	cloves garlic, halved
1	quart tomato juice
2	tablespoons lemon juice
2	tablespoons olive oil
1	teaspoon salt
1/4	teaspoon pepper
1/4	teaspoon hot sauce
1	medium green pepper, seeded and finely chopped
1	medium cucumber, peeled, seeded and finely chopped
1	cup garlic-herb croutons

Place tomatoes, celery, onion and garlic in food processor and finely chop by using a pulse action. Pour vegetables into a large bowl.

Add tomato juice, lemon juice, olive oil, salt, pepper and hot sauce to vegetable mixture, stirring to combine. Cover and refrigerate until chilled. (May be refrigerated for 7 days.)

Stir well before serving. Garnish with green pepper, cucumber and croutons.

Does your family have favorite cold soups? If so, share a recipe here and tell how long you've been making it and where you learned the recipe.

EASY BRUNSWICK STEW

YIELD: *4 to 6 servings*

Jo Anne Coleman
Conyers, Georgia

1	pound ground chuck
1	teaspoon salt
½	teaspoon ground black pepper
1	14.5-ounce can diced tomatoes in sauce
2	medium potatoes, diced
1	large onion, diced
1	tablespoon Worcestershire sauce
1	tablespoon pepper sauce OR 1 tablespoon vinegar and 4 drops hot sauce
1	15-ounce can whole kernel corn, drained
	Hot sauce, optional

In a large skillet, combine ground chuck, salt and pepper. Cook until beef is browned. Drain well. Add remaining ingredients except corn and hot sauce. Bring to a boil; reduce heat and simmer, covered, 45 minutes. Add corn and cook 5 minutes.

Add hot sauce to taste.

GOLDEN RUTABAGA SOUP

YIELD: *4 to 6 servings*

Woody Royster
Columbus, Georgia

1	pound rutabaga, peeled and cubed
1 ½	cups water
2	teaspoons salt, divided
1	pound potatoes, peeled and cubed
½	teaspoon sugar
2	cups milk
2	tablespoons butter or margarine
	Few dashes ground black pepper
1	tablespoon chopped parsley

Place rutabaga, water and 1 teaspoon salt in large pot. Cover tightly, heat to boiling, reduce heat and simmer 20 to 25 minutes. Add potato; cover and cook until potato and rutabaga are fork tender. Mash with a potato masher until fluffy. Add remaining 1 teaspoon salt, sugar, milk, butter and pepper. Heat to boiling; garnish with chopped parsley.

"Great for a cold winter day in Georgia!"
—Woody Royster

This has a very definite rutabaga taste, so you'll either love it or hate it!

Chicken stock can be substituted for water.

Fresh summer vegetables can be substituted for any or all of the vegetables in this recipe. Choose what is abundant and use approximately the same amounts.

HEARTY VEGETABLE SOUP (PICTURED ON PAGE 47)

YIELD: *12 cups*

2	32-ounce cartons chicken broth
1	28-ounce can diced tomatoes
1	cup chopped onion
1	cup diced potatoes
1	cup sliced carrots
1	10-ounce package frozen baby lima beans
1	10-ounce package frozen whole kernel corn
2	teaspoons salt
½	teaspoon pepper
1	bay leaf

Combine all ingredients in a Dutch oven; bring to a boil. Reduce heat, and simmer 1 hour or until vegetables are tender.

MEATBALL STEW

YIELD: *6 to 8 servings*

Fred Kline
Albany, Georgia

1/2	cup quick cooking oats
1/2	cup milk
1/4	cup grated onion
	Salt and pepper to taste
1/4	teaspoon crumbled dried sweet basil or marjoram
1 1/2	pounds ground beef
2	tablespoons butter or margarine
1	tablespoon vegetable oil
1/3	cup all-purpose flour
4	cups beef broth
1	bay leaf
1	clove garlic, crushed
4	medium potatoes, peeled and quartered
5	medium carrots, quartered
1	20-ounce package frozen green beans
2	cups sliced fresh mushrooms

To form meatballs, combine oats, milk, onion, salt, pepper and basil. Add ground beef and mix well. Shape to form 18 meatballs; brown in hot butter and oil in large skillet. Remove meatballs and drain excess fat from skillet.

Combine flour and beef broth; whisk to remove any lumps. Add broth to skillet. Cook over medium heat until thickened, stirring constantly. Add bay leaf, garlic, potatoes, carrots, green beans, mushrooms and meatballs. Bring to a boil. Cover and simmer 30 minutes or until vegetables are tender.

This is a hearty soup and very rich. Frozen meatballs can be substituted: omit the browning step, combine butter and oil, stir in flour to make paste, then add broth to thicken. Proceed with remainder of recipe. Canned mushrooms can be used.

Linda C. Scott
LaGrange, Georgia

OVEN BEEF STEW

YIELD: *6 to 8 servings*

1	28-ounce can crushed tomatoes
2/3	cup dry red wine
1/2	cup beef broth
1/4	cup quick cooking tapioca
1	tablespoon sugar
2	teaspoons dried fines herbes
2	teaspoons salt
2	bay leaves
1/2	teaspoon pepper
3	pounds lean boneless beef, cubed
1	pound carrots, peeled and quartered
4	large ribs celery, cut in 1-inch chunks
3	medium onions, peeled and cut in large chunks

Preheat oven to 325°.

Combine ingredients in a large Dutch oven. Bake for 3 hours or until meat is tender and sauce is thickened. Discard bay leaves before serving.

This stew is best when made a few days ahead and refrigerated.

Possible substitutions: 2/3 cup beef broth for the red wine

2 tablespoons instant blending flour for the tapioca

1 teaspoon each dried thyme, oregano and parsley for fines herbes

SAVORY NAVY BEAN SOUP

YIELD: *7 cups*

1	16-ounce package dried navy beans
6	cups water
2	slices bacon, chopped
½	cup diced onion
2	cloves garlic, minced
1	cup sliced carrots
1	cup sliced celery
1 ½	teaspoon salt
¼	teaspoon white pepper
¼	teaspoon red pepper
1	tablespoon sherry, optional

Sort and wash beans; place in a Dutch oven. Add 6 cups water; cover and soak 8 hours.

Bring mixture to a boil; reduce heat and simmer 1 ½ hours, stirring occasionally. Remove from heat. Place about ⅓ of bean mixture in container of blender; cover and process until smooth. Return to Dutch oven.

Sauté bacon, onion, and garlic in small frying pan until bacon is crisp; drain. Add bacon mixture and remaining ingredients to beans. Cover and simmer an additional 25 minutes. Add more water if thinner soup is desired.

When preparing dried beans, seasoning beans with salt after cooking will help prevent the beans from being tough.

This spicy soup is quick to make for a hungry crowd.

Teenagers are sure to love the familiar flavors of green chiles and spices.

SPICY CHICKEN SOUP

YIELD: *14 cups*

4	chicken breast halves, skinned, boned and cut into bite-size pieces
1	large onion, chopped
1	tablespoon vegetable oil
2	10-ounce cans diced tomatoes and green chiles
1	10-ounce can Mexican tomatoes and green chiles
1	19-ounce can red kidney beans, rinsed and drained
1	15.5-ounce can black beans, rinsed and drained
1	15.5-ounce can whole kernel corn, drained
2	14.5-ounce cans chicken broth
1	teaspoon sugar
½	teaspoon salt
⅓	cup chopped fresh cilantro
	Sour cream, optional
	Shredded Monterey Jack cheese, optional
	Tortilla chips, optional

Sauté chicken and chopped onion in hot oil in Dutch oven over medium-high heat; stir in tomatoes and next 8 ingredients. Bring to a boil over medium-high heat, stirring often. Cover, reduce heat, and simmer 30 minutes.

Sprinkle with cilantro before serving. Garnish with sour cream, shredded cheese or tortilla chips, if desired.

SUMMER GARDEN MINESTRONE

YIELD: *10 cups*

2	teaspoons olive oil
1	cup chopped onion
2	teaspoons chopped fresh oregano
4	cloves garlic, minced
3	cups chopped yellow squash
3	cups chopped zucchini
1	cup chopped carrot
1	cup fresh corn kernels (about 2 ears)
4	cups chopped tomato, divided
3	14-ounce cans chicken broth, divided
½	cup small elbow macaroni
1	15.5-ounce can great northern beans, rinsed and drained
1	6-ounce package fresh baby spinach
1	teaspoon salt
½	teaspoon pepper
1	cup grated fresh Parmesan cheese

Heat oil in Dutch oven over medium-high heat; add onion, and sauté 3 minutes or until softened. Add oregano and garlic; sauté 1 minute. Stir in yellow squash, zucchini, carrot and corn; sauté 5 minutes or until vegetables are tender. Remove from heat.

Place 3 cups tomato and 1 can broth in blender; process until smooth. Add tomato mixture to Dutch oven; return to heat. Stir in remaining 1 cup tomato and remaining 2 cans broth. Bring mixture to a boil. Reduce heat, and simmer 20 minutes.

Add pasta and beans; cook 10 minutes or until pasta is tender, stirring occasionally.

Remove from heat; stir in spinach, salt and pepper. Ladle soup into serving bowls; top with cheese.

Use your Bundt pan or tube pan when cutting fresh corn kernels off the cob. Simply place the pan empty side up and stand the corncob in the tube opening. Hold the top end of the cob with your hand and cut straight down. The corn kernels and juices will fall into the pan below.

Hungry teenagers can prepare Taco Stew and customize their bowls with tasty toppings. Set out side dishes of sour cream, grated cheese and green onions.

TACO STEW

YIELD: *4 to 6 servings*

Ester Case
Dawsonville, Georgia

1	pound lean ground beef
1	medium onion, chopped
1	15.5-ounce can whole kernel corn, undrained
1	10-ounce can chili beans in spicy sauce, undrained
1	1.5-ounce envelope taco seasoning mix
1	10¾-ounce can tomato soup, undiluted
1	cup water
	Tortilla Chips
	Monterey Jack cheese, grated

Brown ground beef and onion in Dutch oven. Combine remaining ingredients, except chips and cheese. Simmer on low for 30 minutes, stirring frequently.

To serve, place tortilla chips in bottom of bowl and cover with a generous helping of stew. Top with cheese.

White Bean Chili

Maria Sanchez
Gainesville, Georgia

YIELDS: *10 cups*

4	skinless, boneless chicken breast halves
2	medium onions, chopped
2	cloves garlic, minced
1	tablespoon vegetable oil
2	14½-ounce cans chicken broth
3	15-ounce cans great northern or cannelloni beans, rinsed and drained
1	15-ounce can cannelloni beans, drained and mashed
1	4½-ounce can chopped green chilies
1	teaspoon salt
¾	teaspoon dried oregano
1	teaspoon ground cumin
½	teaspoon chili powder
⅛	teaspoon ground red pepper
	Toppings: Sour cream, shredded cheese, chopped fresh cilantro

Cut chicken into bite-size pieces. Sauté chicken, onion and garlic in hot oil in a Dutch oven over medium-high heat for 10 minutes or until chicken is done. Stir in broth and next 10 ingredients; bring to a boil. Cover, reduce heat and simmer 30 minutes. Serve with desired toppings.

A great alternative to traditional chili with similar flavors. Spices can be adjusted to taste.

You will want to include this delicious chili on your menu when serving a crowd — whether your guests are teammates or Christmas carolers, bowling buddies or bridge partners.

SIDES

When recounting a memorable meal, a Southerner will of course mention the main entrèe, but words will flow abundantly when describing the side dishes. Sides are to a Southern meal what rainbows are to rain showers. Their presence is anticipated and often hailed.

Your family and friends will appreciate your efforts to include new side dishes during your gatherings. Why not start by offering them Carrot Souffle *(pg. 105)* or Cheese Apples *(pg. 106)*?

Onion Pudding *(pg. 113)* is sure to impress, and Layered Tomato Casserole *(pg. 112)* will complement a broad range of main dishes. With this many side recipes all in one section, it's your time to prove there is no room on the table for boring sides. It's too much fun trying new flavors and combinations.

CANDIED SWEET POTATOES

YIELD: *4 servings*

Kelley Turk
Atlanta, Georgia

2	large Georgia sweet potatoes (about 2 pounds), peeled
1/4	cup orange juice
2	tablespoons firmly packed light brown sugar
2	tablespoons maple syrup
1	tablespoon melted margarine
1/2	teaspoon salt

Preheat oven to 375°.

Cut potatoes in half lengthwise, then crosswise into 2-inch thick pieces. Place sweet potatoes in large saucepan with just enough water to cover. Bring to a boil over high heat; reduce heat and simmer until potatoes are fork tender (about 10 minutes). Drain potatoes and place in a single layer in a shallow baking dish.

Whisk together remaining ingredients. Pour mixture over potatoes. Bake for 30 minutes. Stir to coat potatoes with liquid and bake 15 minutes more until sauce is thick and bubbly.

CARROT SOUFFLÉ

YIELD: *4 to 6 servings*

Minnie L. Tiller
Athens, Georgia

1	pound carrots, peeled and chopped
3	eggs, lightly beaten
1/2	cup sugar
1/2	cup melted butter
3	tablespoons all-purpose flour
1	teaspoon baking powder
1	teaspoon vanilla extract

Place carrots in a medium saucepan, add water to cover and bring to a boil. Cook covered for 45 minutes or until carrots are fork tender. Drain.

Preheat oven to 350°.

Process carrots in food processor until smooth. Stir together carrot purée and remaining ingredients. Spoon into a lightly greased 1-quart baking dish. Bake for 45 minutes or until set. Serve immediately.

This recipe is for those folks who don't like carrots! It could almost be served as a dessert.

You can substitute sweet potatoes for carrots.

A great brunch dish that is not sweet and goes well with eggs.

CHEESE APPLES

YIELD: *8-10 servings*

Georgia Apple Commission

10	Georgia Granny Smith apples (or any tart apple), peeled, cored and thinly sliced
	Juice of 1 lemon
$1/4$	cup sugar
$1/4$	cup water
$1\,1/2$	cups all-purpose flour
$1/2$	cup sugar
8	ounces sharp New York Cheddar cheese, shredded
1	stick butter, cut into pieces

Preheat oven to 350°.

Combine sliced apples, lemon juice, $1/4$ cup sugar and water in 9-x13-inch baking dish. Set aside.

Combine flour, $1/2$ cup sugar and shredded cheese in medium mixing bowl. Cut butter into mixture with pastry blender. Or place all ingredients in bowl of food processor and process until well blended.

Sprinkle cheese mixture over apples. Bake for 45 minutes to 1 hour.

Serve warm.

CHEESE GRITS

YIELD: *8 servings*

4	cups cold water
1	teaspoon salt
1	cup uncooked quick-cooking grits (not instant)
2	cups (8-ounces) shredded extra sharp Cheddar cheese
3/4	cup milk
1/4	cup butter
1	teaspoon Worcestershire sauce
1/4	teaspoon dry mustard
1/4	teaspoon ground red pepper
4	eggs, lightly beaten
1/4	teaspoon paprika

Preheat oven to 350°.

Bring water and salt to boil in a large saucepan; stir in grits. Return to boil. Cover; reduce heat and simmer 5 minutes, stirring occasionally. Remove from heat; add cheese, milk and butter, stirring to melt cheese and butter. Add remaining ingredients; stir well.

Spoon mixture into lightly greased 2-quart baking dish; sprinkle with paprika. Bake, uncovered, for 1 hour. Let stand 5 minutes before serving.

"Like most Southerners, I love my grits at breakfast with butter or gravy. I've learned to reduce the fat by adding a serving of egg substitute for each serving of grits while the grits are cooking. This gives them a beautiful buttery yellow color, and adds flavor and extra nutrition without adding fat."

— *Joanna Patterson*
Duluth, Georgia

COMPANY SQUASH CASSEROLE

Martha Wood
Conyers, Georgia

YIELD: *4 to 6 servings*

1	pound yellow squash, cooked and mashed
½	cup chopped onion
1	cup grated extra sharp cheese
1	teaspoon sugar
½	teaspoon salt
¼	teaspoon ground black pepper
½	cup mayonnaise
1	egg, beaten
1	stick butter, melted
1	sleeve round buttery crackers, crushed

Preheat oven to 350°.

Combine squash, onion, cheese, sugar, salt, pepper, mayonnaise and egg in a large mixing bowl. Stir to mix well. Pour into a greased 2-quart baking dish.

Combine melted butter and crushed crackers in a medium mixing bowl. Stir with a fork to combine.

Sprinkle cracker mixture over casserole. Bake for 35 to 40 minutes.

CRUNCHY GREEN BEANS WITH CARAMELIZED VIDALIA ONIONS

YIELD: *4 servings*

1	pound fresh green beans, ends removed
¼	teaspoon salt
2	medium Vidalia onions, thinly sliced
1	tablespoon firmly packed brown sugar
2	teaspoons vinegar (cider, red wine or balsamic)

Cook green beans in boiling salted water for 10 minutes or until bright green and crisp-tender. Rinse under cold water; drain and set aside.

Cook onion in large non-stick skillet over medium-high heat for 15 to 20 minutes, stirring often until onions are golden brown. Reduce heat to medium; add brown sugar and vinegar. Stir to combine. Add green beans and heat 5 minutes or until beans are heated through.

CRUNCHY GREEN BEANS WITH PECANS (PICTURED ON PAGE 18)

YIELD: *4 servings*

1	pound fresh green beans, ends removed
1/4	teaspoon salt
1	tablespoon melted butter
1/4	cup chopped and toasted Georgia pecans

Cook green beans in boiling salted water for 10 minutes or until bright green and crisp-tender. Rinse under cold water; drain and set aside.

Place melted butter in large non-stick skillet. Add beans and heat through. Stir in pecans. Serve warm.

CRUNCHY GREEN BEANS WITH ROSEMARY, PECANS AND LEMON

YIELD: *4 servings*

1	pound fresh green beans, ends removed
1/4	teaspoon salt
1	tablespoon olive oil
1/4	cup sliced green onions
1/4	cup chopped and toasted Georgia pecans
2	teaspoons finely chopped fresh rosemary OR 1 teaspoon dried rosemary
2	teaspoons fresh lemon juice
2	teaspoons grated lemon zest

Cook green beans in boiling salted water for 10 minutes or until bright green and crisp-tender. Rinse under cold water; drain and set aside.

Heat olive oil in large skillet over medium heat. Add green onions and cook, stirring constantly, about 3 minutes. Add green beans, pecans, rosemary and lemon juice; cook, stirring constantly until mixture is heated. Sprinkle with lemon zest.

To enhance this dish, add 1/2 cup chopped sweet red pepper or 1/4 cup crumbled blue cheese to the Green Beans with Pecans before serving.

Kids love to create in the kitchen, and most children like Mac and Cheese. Do you encourage your children or grandchildren to cook with you? Do you have a special macaroni and cheese recipe they like?

DELUXE MACARONI & CHEESE

Martha Phillips
Barnesville, Georgia

YIELD: 6 TO 8 *servings*

1	8-ounce box elbow macaroni, cooked and drained
1	10-ounce can cream of chicken soup
1	cup mayonnaise
1	small onion, chopped
1	2-ounce jar chopped pimento
2	cups shredded sharp Cheddar cheese
1	2.8-ounce can French fried onions

Preheat oven to 350°.

Combine all ingredients except fried onions in a large mixing bowl.

Pour into a 2-quart baking dish. Bake for 30 to 35 minutes or until bubbly. Top with fried onions and bake an additional 5 minutes.

EGGPLANT PROVENÇAL

YIELD: *10 to 12 servings*

2	tablespoons olive oil
3/4	cup chopped onion
4	cups eggplant, peeled and cut into 1-inch cubes
2	cups chopped green pepper
3	cups sliced yellow squash (or zucchini)
2	cloves garlic, minced
1	teaspoon dried thyme
1	bay leaf
3	tomatoes, peeled, cored and chopped
	Salt and pepper to taste

Heat oil in large skillet over high heat. Add onion and sauté until golden. Add remaining ingredients. Cover, lower heat and simmer for 45 minutes. Uncover and continue to cook for 15 minutes or until liquid is reduced.

GARDEN VEGETABLE CASSEROLE

YIELD: *4 to 6 servings*

Bessie Simmons
Cordele, Georgia

⅓	cup long grain white rice, uncooked
4 or 5	small yellow squash, thinly sliced
2	medium onions, thinly sliced
1	green pepper, thinly sliced
4 or 5	tomatoes, peeled and sliced
	Salt and pepper to taste
2	tablespoons butter

Preheat oven to 325°.

Grease a 2-quart baking dish. Arrange vegetables and rice in layers. Place one third of the vegetables on the bottom of the dish; add all the rice. Continue layering vegetables, salt, pepper and butter ending with tomatoes. Tomatoes should completely cover top layer. Cover tightly with foil. Bake for 1 ½ hours.

GREEN CHILE CHEESE CORN CASSEROLE

YIELD: *8 servings*

Suzanne McNeely
Hoboken, Georgia

2	eggs, lightly beaten
1 ½	cups sour cream
2	cups fresh corn kernels
2	cups (8-ounces) shredded Monterey Jack cheese
½	cup soft breadcrumbs
1	4.5-ounce can chopped green chiles, drained
½	teaspoon salt
¼	teaspoon pepper
½	cup (2-ounces) shredded Cheddar cheese

Preheat oven to 350°.

Combine eggs and sour cream in large mixing bowl; stir in corn and next 5 ingredients. Pour into a greased 2-quart baking dish. Bake for 30 minutes. Sprinkle with Cheddar cheese, and bake an additional 5 minutes. Remove from oven and let stand 10 minutes before serving.

A great way to use an abundance of summer squash!

Try adding ½ teaspoon dried thyme to the vegetables. Those watching their carbohydrates can eliminate the rice.

Leftovers — if there are any — are good eaten cold.

LAYERED TOMATO CASSEROLE

Hilda Jernigan
Dalton, Georgia

YIELD: *4 to 6 servings*

4 or 5	medium tomatoes, seeded and sliced
1	medium Vidalia onion, chopped
½	medium green pepper, chopped
½	medium red sweet pepper, chopped
	Salt and pepper to taste
½	cup grated Parmesan cheese
½	cup grated sharp cheese
1	cup mayonnaise

Preheat oven to 350°.

Layer tomatoes, onion and peppers in 2-quart baking dish, seasoning each layer with salt and pepper. Combine cheeses and mayonnaise. Spread over top of vegetable layers. Bake for 45 minutes.

LOW-FAT BROCCOLI RICE CASSEROLE

YIELD: *6 servings*

1	10-ounce package frozen chopped broccoli, cooked and drained
2	cups cooked rice
1	10-ounce can fat-free cream of chicken soup
1	8-ounce container light processed cheese food
2	tablespoons chopped onion
	Salt and pepper to taste

Preheat oven to 350°.

Combine all ingredients in a large mixing bowl; stir to combine. Pour into a greased 2-quart baking dish. Bake for 30 minutes or until mixture is hot and bubbly.

ONION PUDDING

YIELD: *8 to 10 servings*

Rosie Higgins
Lawrenceville, Georgia

1	tablespoon margarine
3	cups chopped onion
4	cups broth (chicken, beef or vegetable)
1	12-ounce French bread baguette (8 cups bread cubes)
2	cups shredded Swiss cheese

Preheat oven to 300°.

Melt margarine in large skillet. Add onions and cook until caramelized (about 5 minutes). Combine onions and broth, set aside.

Tear French bread into small pieces; place in greased 13x9-inch glass dish. Pour onion mixture over bread; top with shredded cheese. Bake for 30 minutes.

This is a nice accompaniment to roast beef and is similar in taste to French onion soup. The texture is very soft, but it holds up well on the plate. It would be delicious prepared with Vidalias.

POTATO CASSEROLE

YIELD: *8 to 10 servings*

Minnie L. Tiller
Athens, Georgia

1	30-ounce package frozen shredded hash brown potatoes, thawed
2	cups sour cream
2	cups shredded sharp Cheddar cheese
1	10¾-ounce can cream of chicken soup, undiluted
½	cup chopped onions
¼	cup melted butter
2	tablespoons chopped fresh parsley
½	teaspoon ground black pepper
¼	teaspoon salt

Preheat oven to 350°.

Combine all ingredients in a large mixing bowl. Place in a greased 2 quart baking dish. Bake for 1 hour or until heated through.

"This is a tried-and-true recipe and always a holiday favorite."

— *Minnie L. Tiller*

What favorite dishes do you like to make for covered dish suppers? Please include the recipes here and any tips you would like to share.

Roasted Asparagus (PICTURED ON PAGE 22)

YIELD: *4 servings*

1	pound fresh asparagus
1	tablespoon oil
1	tablespoon grated lemon rind
	Salt and pepper to taste

Preheat oven to 375°.

Snap off tough ends of asparagus. Arrange asparagus in single layer in a 13x9-inch baking pan. Drizzle with oil; sprinkle with lemon rind. Add salt and pepper to taste. Bake for 8 to 10 minutes or until asparagus is crisp tender, shaking pan occasionally.

Sautéed Apples and Bacon (PICTURED ON PAGE 37)

YIELD: *4 servings*

8	slices bacon
4	cups peeled, cored and cubed tart Georgia apples
2	teaspoons oil
2	tablespoons firmly packed light brown sugar

Cook bacon in large heavy skillet; drain, reserving 2 tablespoons drippings. Crumble bacon and set aside.

Combine oil and reserved bacon drippings in skillet; add apples. Sauté, uncovered, over high heat until translucent. Sprinkle with sugar and crumbled bacon.

Skillet Cabbage

M. P. Whatley
Lilburn, Georgia

YIELD: *4 servings*

1	tablespoon vegetable oil
3	cups finely shredded cabbage
1	cup chopped celery
1	small green pepper, seeded and chopped
1/2	teaspoon salt
	Dash ground black pepper

Place large skillet over medium heat; add oil. Add remaining ingredients and stir well. Cover and cook 5 minutes, stirring occasionally. Serve immediately.

Vegetables will be crisp and crunchy.

This does need to be served immediately!

Squash Dressing

Marian Cofer

YIELD: *8 servings*

2	cups cooked, drained and mashed yellow squash (or zucchini)
2	cups crumbled cornbread
1	10^{3}/$_{4}$-ounce can cream of chicken soup
1	small onion, chopped
1/2	cup margarine, melted
	Crumbled sage to taste (start with 1/2 teaspoon)
	Salt and pepper to taste
3	large eggs, lightly beaten

Preheat oven to 350°.

Combine first 5 ingredients. Add seasonings to taste. Stir in eggs; pour into lightly greased 2-quart baking dish. Bake for 40 to 45 minutes.

When yellow squash is abundant, try this delicious dressing. It is a good way to use left-over cooked squash and leftover cornbread.

If you do not have left-over squash and cornbread, about 8 small squash cooked in boiling, salted water will yield 2 cups of cooked squash.

A 7-ounce package of cornbread mix baked in an 8-inch square pan makes exactly 2 cups of crumbs.

Why not try this dish on New Year's Day in place of customary collard greens? Or serve Turnip Green Casserole throughout the year to welcome prosperity.

TURNIP GREEN CASSEROLE

YIELD: *8 servings*

2	cups cooked turnip greens
½	cup chopped onion
1	10-ounce can cream of mushroom soup
½	cup mayonnaise
1	teaspoon horseradish
1	teaspoon sugar
3	tablespoons white wine vinegar
3	eggs, beaten
1	teaspoon salt
½	teaspoon pepper
1	cup fresh breadcrumbs
1	cup shredded sharp Cheddar cheese

Preheat oven to 350°.

Combine turnip greens, onion, soup, mayonnaise, horseradish, sugar, vinegar, eggs, salt and pepper in a large mixing bowl. Stir well to combine. Spoon mixture into a greased 2-quart baking dish. Bake for 30 minutes.

Combine breadcrumbs and cheese in a small bowl. Sprinkle over casserole. Return to oven and bake until cheese melts and crumbs are lightly browned.

WARM GRAPE TOMATOES

YIELD: *4 to 6 servings*

Rachael Russell
Valdosta, Georgia

2	tablespoons extra virgin olive oil
2	cloves fresh garlic, minced
2	pints grape tomatoes
6	green onions, sliced
2	tablespoons red wine vinegar
	Salt and pepper to taste
½	cup chopped parsley
¼	cup chopped fresh basil

Add olive oil to a large skillet. Place over medium heat. Add garlic, tomatoes, onions, and cook until tomato skins burst. Remove from heat and add remaining ingredients. Toss and serve immediately.

This is a quick-and-easy side dish that can be prepared at the last minute and goes with any meal.

Be sure to use fresh basil. You can substitute cherry tomatoes for grape tomatoes and Vidalia onion for the green onions.

MAIN DISHES

Preheat your oven or fire up the grill because your mouth won't want to wait after you read these Main Dish recipes. You'll savor the flavors of Apple Barbecued Ribs *(pg. 118)* while planning your next meal around Crisp Fried Catfish *(pg. 128)*.

Tasting Pecan Trout *(pg. 137)* and Buttermilk Fried Chicken *(pg. 122)* will remind you that "mouth-watering" is an accurate term. Southern hospitality will forever be in style when you serve Herbed Turkey Breast *(pg. 130)* or Shrimp and Crab Casserole *(pg. 141)*.

Planning a cookout? Try the Grilled Lemon and Oregano Chicken Breasts *(pg. 129)*. Or, involve your guests by hosting a hands-on Low Country Boil *(p. 134)*. Whatever you try first, know that many more recipes for Main Dishes are available for preparing and sharing.

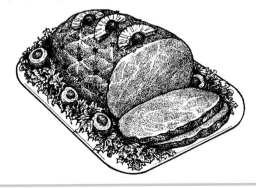

When buying ribs, fig-ure on about 1 pound per person.

APPLE BARBECUED RIBS   (PICTURED ON PAGE 31)

YIELD: *4-6 servings*

5-6	pounds spareribs
4	quarts water
$\frac{1}{2}$	cup chopped onion
$\frac{1}{4}$	cup vegetable oil
$\frac{1}{2}$	cup ketchup
$\frac{1}{3}$	cup chopped fresh parsley
2	tablespoons honey
2	tablespoons lemon juice
1	tablespoon Worcestershire sauce
1	teaspoon salt
1	teaspoon prepared mustard
$\frac{1}{2}$	teaspoon ground ginger
$\frac{1}{4}$	teaspoon pepper
1	clove garlic, minced
1	pint applesauce

Cut ribs into serving size pieces; place in large Dutch oven. Add water; cover and simmer 20 to 30 minutes.

Sauté onion in hot oil in medium saucepan until tender. Add next 11 ingredients; simmer 15 minutes.

Remove ribs from Dutch oven. Place on grill over slow coals. Baste with sauce. Grill approximately 40 minutes, turning frequently. Serve with remaining sauce.

BAKED HAM

YIELD: *15 to 20 servings*

Mr. and Mrs.
Edward S. Morrow
Marietta, Georgia

1	7- to 10-pound fully cooked ham
½ - ¾	cup water
1	1-pound box light brown sugar
1	20-ounce can sliced pineapple, reserve juice
2 - 3	tablespoons pineapple juice
1	10-ounce jar maraschino cherries

Preheat oven to 300°.

Trim fat from ham. Wrap ham in aluminum foil and place in baking pan with ½ to ¾ cup water in bottom of pan. Bake for 25 minutes per pound or until meat thermometer registers 140°. Ham will be fork tender. Drain juice from ham.

Combine brown sugar and pineapple juice to make a thick paste. Spoon mixture over ham. With foil open, return ham to oven for 1 hour or until light brown. Place pineapple slices and cherries over ham; baste with pan juices and bake until pineapple begins to brown, approximately 20 to 30 minutes.

The aroma of ham baking in the oven makes any day a special occasion.

Add leftover ham tidbits to Deluxe Macaroni & Cheese (pg. 110), Breakfast Casserole (pg. 121) or Cheese Grits (pg. 107).

When serving slices of Country Ham, Red Eye Gravy is a must. It is easy to make. Just add ¼ cup strong coffee and 1 cup water to the pan drippings left from frying the country ham; heat and stir to loosen browned bits and serve with ham and Cheese Grits (pg. 107).

To make Oven Barbecued Chicken, pour sauce over chicken in large baking pan. Bake, covered, at 350° for 1 hour or until chicken is tender. Uncover, baste with sauce and broil 10 to 15 minutes.

BARBECUED CHICKEN WITH BASIC BARBECUE SAUCE

YIELD: *10 to 12 servings*

3	2- to 2 1/2-pound boiler-fryers, quartered
1/4	cup melted butter
	Basic Barbecue Sauce (or commercial sauce)

Preheat grill. Place chicken, skin side down, over medium heat. Brown about 10 minutes, then turn chicken skin side up. Brush with melted butter. Repeat procedure every 10 minutes for 30 minutes.

After 30 minutes, baste with 1 cup Basic Barbecue Sauce. Cook 10 minutes or until sauce browns. Serve remaining sauce on the side.

Basic Barbecue Sauce

YIELD: *2 1/2 cups*

1/2	cup cider vinegar
1	cup water
4	tablespoons sugar
2	teaspoons black pepper
2	teaspoons salt
2	tablespoons prepared mustard
1/4	teaspoon red pepper
2	tablespoons lemon juice
1 1/2	cups ketchup
4	tablespoons Worcestershire sauce

Combine first 8 ingredients in a medium saucepan over low heat. Simmer for 20 minutes. Add ketchup and Worcestershire. Bring to a boil.

Remove from heat. Baste meat with sauce during last 10 to 15 minutes of cooking time or cool sauce and store in refrigerator.

BREAKFAST CASSEROLE (PICTURED ON PAGE 19)

Georgia Egg Commission

YIELD: *6 servings*

10	eggs, lightly beaten
3	cups milk
2	teaspoons dry mustard
1	teaspoon salt
½	teaspoon pepper
6	cups cubed bread
2	cups chopped cooked ham
2	cups (8-ounces) shredded sharp Cheddar cheese
½	cup chopped mushrooms
1	medium tomato, chopped
½	cup sliced green onions

Preheat oven to 325°.

Combine eggs, milk, mustard, salt and pepper in a large mixing bowl; stir well. Place half the bread in a lightly greased 13x9-inch baking dish. Sprinkle with half the ham, half the cheese and half the vegetables. Repeat layers. Pour egg mixture evenly over casserole.

Cover and refrigerate overnight or bake immediately.

Bake 60 minutes or until eggs are set. Tent with foil if top begins to brown too quickly.

Well-suited for morning, this dish is a favorite on brunch buffets and can be reheated for an anytime snack. It's easy to prepare especially if you have leftover ham from the Baked Ham on page 119.

Do not overcrowd the skillet when frying chicken. The oil will cool down too quickly and cause uneven cooking.

BUTTERMILK FRIED CHICKEN   (PICTURED ON PAGE 32)

YIELD: *4 to 6 servings*

1	3- to 3 ½-pound broiler-fryer, cut up
2	cups buttermilk
1	cup self-rising flour
1 ½	teaspoons salt
1	teaspoon pepper
	Vegetable oil

Place chicken in shallow pan and pour buttermilk over top. Cover and refrigerate overnight or at least 8 hours.

Remove chicken from buttermilk. Combine flour, salt and pepper in plastic bag; shake to mix. Place 2 or 3 pieces of chicken in bag and shake well. Repeat procedure with remaining chicken.

Heat 1-inch of oil in a large skillet to 325°; add chicken and fry 25 minutes or until golden brown, turning once. Drain on paper towels.

CAJUN GOURMET BEER BURGER

YIELD: *8-10 servings*

Ronald Treadaway, Sr.
Acworth, Georgia

1	egg, lightly beaten
1/4	cup beer or ale
2	tablespoons fine dry bread crumbs
2	tablespoons Worcestershire sauce
1	tablespoon soy sauce
1/4	teaspoon bottled hot pepper sauce
1/4	teaspoon salt
1/4	teaspoon black pepper
1/4	teaspoon dry mustard
1/4	teaspoon seasoned salt
1/4	teaspoon crushed dried thyme
1/4	teaspoon cornstarch
1	large onion, chopped
1	medium green pepper, chopped
3/4	cup finely chopped green onions
4	cloves garlic, minced
2	pounds ground chuck or ground sirloin

Combine egg and beer in a large mixing bowl. Stir in remaining ingredients in order listed. Mix well. Shape meat into 8 (3/4-inch) thick patties or 10 (1/2-inch thick) patties.

Grill patties over medium coals for 14 to18 minutes or until no pink remains, turning once.

A steaming bowl of Chicken and Dumplings with a big square of Southern Style Buttermilk Cornbread (p. 73) can't be beat on a cold winter day!

Whether your favorite is "slick" dumplings as in this recipe or "fluffy" dumplings, this is one of those old-time Southern dishes enjoyed by all generations.

CHICKEN AND DUMPLINGS

YIELD: *6 servings*

1	3- to 4-pound broiler-fryer
1	large onion, halved
1	stalk celery, halved
1 ½	teaspoons salt
½	teaspoon pepper
2	quarts water
2	cups all-purpose flour
1	teaspoon salt
2	tablespoons shortening
½	cup hot water
⅓	cup all-purpose flour

Combine chicken, onion, celery, salt, pepper and water in a large Dutch oven; bring to a boil. Cover, reduce heat, and simmer 1 hour or until chicken is tender.

Remove chicken from broth; cool. Strain broth. Bone chicken and cut meat into bite-size pieces. Return chicken to broth; set aside.

Combine 2 cups flour and 1 teaspoon salt; cut in shortening with a pastry blender until mixture resembles coarse meal. Stir in hot water with a fork until dry ingredients are moistened. Turn dough onto a lightly floured surface. Roll dough to $\frac{1}{16}$-inch thickness; cut into 1x3-inch strips. Bring chicken broth to a boil. Drop dumpling strips into broth. Cover; reduce heat, and simmer 20 minutes or until dumplings are plump and tender. Remove chicken and dumplings to a large serving bowl.

Blend $\frac{1}{3}$ cup flour with a small amount of water, mixing to form a thick paste; add to broth, stirring until smooth. Cook, stirring constantly, until thickened and bubbly. Pour sauce over chicken and dumplings in serving dish.

CHICKEN AND MUSHROOM TETRAZZINI (PICTURED ON PAGE 40)

YIELD: *8-10 servings*

1	7-ounce package thin spaghetti, cooked and drained
1	8-ounce package sliced fresh mushrooms, sautéed
½	cup butter, melted
2	cups cooked and chopped chicken breast
1	10¾-ounce can cream of chicken soup
1	10¾-ounce can cream of mushroom soup
1	16-ounce carton sour cream
1	cup shredded Cheddar cheese (reserve ½ cup for topping)
¼	cup sherry or white wine, optional

Preheat oven to 350°.

Combine all ingredients in a large mixing bowl. Stir to combine.

Spoon into a 2-quart baking dish. Bake for 25 to 30 minutes or until casserole is bubbly and heated through. Sprinkle with remaining cheese.

Bake 5 additional minutes.

This freezes well before baking or as leftovers.

Planning a party? Try preparing this dish in advance. Follow recipe but do not bake casserole. Wrap the tetrazzini before freezing. When ready to cook, remove dish from freezer and allow one hour of room temperature thawing time. Unwrap and follow recipe directions.

Substitute chicken broth for sherry, if desired.

A can of cream of mushroom soup can be substituted for the white sauce.

CHICKEN DIVAN POT PIE

YIELD: *6 servings*

3	tablespoons butter or margarine
3	tablespoons all-purpose flour
1/4	teaspoon ground black pepper
1/2	cup chicken broth
1/4	cup milk
1	cup (4-ounces) shredded American cheese
2	cups cooked and diced chicken
1	10-ounce package frozen chopped broccoli, thawed, drained well
1	12-ounce package deep dish frozen pie crusts (2 per package)

Preheat oven to 425˚.

Place cookie sheet in oven to preheat. In a medium saucepan, combine butter, flour and pepper. Cook over low heat until mixture becomes thick and bubbly. Gradually stir in broth and milk. Stir until mixture begins to thicken; add cheese and stir until melted. Stir in chicken and broccoli. Pour mixture into pie crust.

Remove second crust from pie pan and center frozen crust upright on top of filled pie. Let thaw 10 to 20 minutes and crimp edges together. Cut three slits in top crust.

Place pie on preheated cookie sheet. Bake for 30 to 35 minutes or until crust is brown and filling is bubbly.

COLA ROAST

YIELD: *8 to 10 servings*

1	4- to 5-pound bottom round roast
½	teaspoon salt
½	teaspoon pepper
½	teaspoon garlic salt
1½	cups cola
1	12-ounce bottle chili sauce
2	tablespoons Worcestershire sauce
2	teaspoons hot sauce (or to taste)

Preheat oven to 325°.

Rub roast with salt, pepper and garlic salt; place in heavy roasting pan.

Mix remaining ingredients; pour over roast. Cover tightly and bake for 3 hours.

Here's a good spot to make notes about your family's favorite pot roast. What vegetables do you add and when? Do you add special spices or seasonings?

Golden Hush Puppies (p. 70) are a traditional favorite to serve with catfish. Self-rising cornmeal is used in both recipes.

Remoulade Sauce is simply a spicier version of traditional tartar sauce.

CRISP FRIED CATFISH WITH REMOULADE SAUCE   (PICTURED ON PAGE 29)

YIELD: *6 servings*

6	small catfish, filleted
1	teaspoon salt
1/4	teaspoon pepper
2	cups self-rising cornmeal
	Vegetable oil
	Remoulade Sauce

Sprinkle catfish with salt and pepper, and coat with cornmeal. Fry fish in hot oil about 4 minutes on each side or until golden brown. Drain on absorbent paper. Serve hot.

Remoulade Sauce

YIELD: *1 3/4 cups*

1 1/2	cups mayonnaise
2	tablespoons Creole mustard
1	tablespoon chopped capers
1	tablespoon chopped sweet pickle
1	tablespoon chopped fresh parsley
1	teaspoon dried tarragon

Combine all ingredients; cover and chill. Serve with Crisp Fried Catfish.

EASY LONDON BROIL (PICTURED ON PAGE 27)

Mrs. Isabelle Hotchkiss
Atlanta, Georgia

YIELD: *6 servings*

½	cup cola
½	cup commercial Italian salad dressing
½	cup vegetable oil
	Juice of 1 lemon
½	cup soy sauce
¼	cup Worcestershire sauce
1	2- to 3-pound London broil or flank steak

Combine all ingredients except steak in a large heavyweight zip-top bag. Add steak; close tightly, refrigerate for 2 to 3 hours. Remove steak from marinade and discard liquid.

Broil steak 3 to 4 inches from heating element for 6 to 7 minutes on each side or until desired doneness.

GRILLED LEMON AND OREGANO CHICKEN BREASTS (PICTURED ON PAGE 34)

YIELD: *4 servings*

4	boneless, skinless chicken breast halves
5	teaspoons grated lemon rind
1	tablespoon olive oil
1½	teaspoons dried oregano
¾	teaspoon salt
½	teaspoon pepper
¼	teaspoon water
2	garlic cloves, minced
4	lemon wedges

Preheat grill.

Place each chicken breast half between 2 sheets of plastic wrap and pound to ¼-inch thickness with meat mallet or rolling pin.

Combine remaining ingredients; rub evenly over both sides of chicken.

Grill chicken 3 minutes on each side or until chicken is done. Squeeze lemon juice over chicken.

This is great for grilling too! Make sure you allow time for the meat to rest before slicing. Resting time gives the juices a chance to redistribute throughout the meat — keeping it moist and juicy.

A whole chicken or bone-in chicken breasts can also be prepared in this manner.

HERBED TURKEY BREAST (PICTURED ON PAGE 39)

YIELD: *12 servings*

3	tablespoons butter
2	tablespoons chopped fresh parsley
$\frac{1}{2}$	teaspoon grated lemon rind
$\frac{1}{4}$	teaspoon dried thyme
$\frac{1}{4}$	teaspoon salt
$\frac{1}{4}$	teaspoon dried sage
$\frac{1}{4}$	teaspoon pepper
1	clove garlic, crushed
1	5- to 5$\frac{1}{2}$-pound bone-in turkey breast

Preheat oven to 325°.

Melt butter; add next 7 ingredients. Rub turkey breast with the mixture and place in a lightly greased baking dish.

Cover loosely with aluminum foil and bake for 1 hour.

Uncover and bake 1 hour more or until a meat thermometer registers 170°, basting every 15 minutes.

King Ranch Chicken Casserole

YIELD: *10 servings*

1	10¾-ounce can cream of chicken soup
1	10¾-ounce can cream of mushroom soup
1	10-ounce can tomatoes and green chiles
2	cups chicken broth
1	12-ounce bag tortilla chips, crushed
2	cups cooked and chopped chicken
1	large onion, chopped
1	medium-size green pepper, chopped
3	cups shredded Cheddar cheese
	Salsa, black olives and sour cream, optional

Preheat oven to 350°.

Combine soups, tomatoes and broth; set aside.

Lightly grease a 3-quart baking dish. Layer half the tortilla chips, chicken, onion, green pepper and cheese. Pour half the soup mixture over. Repeat layers and top with remaining cheese.

Bake for 45 to 60 minutes.

Garnish with salsa, olives and sour cream, if desired.

This recipe can be frozen and baked later. Leftovers also freeze well.

National Pork Producers
Recipe courtesy of *Southern
Living Bar-B-Que: The Ultimate
Guide*

Don't be put off by the length of this recipe. Not only does it include recipes for the rub and sauce, but it also gives step-by-step instructions for cooking mouth-watering pulled pork!

LOW AND SLOW PULLED PORK

YIELD: *12 to14 servings*

| 1 | Boston butt pork roast, about 5 pounds |

Rub

1	cup firmly packed dark brown sugar
½	cup granulated garlic
½	cup kosher salt
½	cup paprika
2	tablespoons granulated onion
1	tablespoon dry mustard
1	tablespoon Creole seasoning
1	tablespoon chili powder
1	tablespoon ground red pepper
1	tablespoon ground cumin
1	tablespoon ground black pepper

Sauce

¾	cup cider vinegar
½	cup ketchup
¼	cup Worcestershire sauce
1	clove garlic, minced
1/4	cup chili sauce
2	tablespoons chopped onion
1	tablespoon brown sugar
1	tablespoon lemon juice
1/2	teaspoon dry mustard
	Dash of ground red pepper

Hardwood chips, soaked in water for 1 hour
Apple juice, for spritzing

Stir together all rub ingredients in a bowl. Store in an airtight container. Set aside.

Stir together all ingredients for the sauce in a medium saucepan over medium heat; bring to a boil. Reduce heat; simmer, stirring occasionally, 40 minutes.

Divide sauce into separate containers for basting and serving at the table. (Basting brushes used on raw food should not be dipped into table sauce.) Use as a basting sauce during the last 10 minutes of cooking for steak, pork, burgers, or chicken. Discard any remaining basting sauce, and refrigerate any leftover table sauce.

If needed, trim the fat to about $\frac{1}{8}$ inch thick. Sprinkle meat generously with rub, massaging it into the meat. Wrap tightly with plastic wrap and refrigerate overnight.

Smoking a large piece of meat takes a long time, so you'll need to get an early start. Prepare your smoker or grill until the temperature reaches 250°. Take the meat out of the refrigerator and let it sit for about 30 to 45 minutes. Having the pork at room temperature is very important, because if you put it on the smoker cold, the outer portion will burn.

Smoke is one of the main ingredients of good barbecue. Soak hickory wood chips (or any other hardwood chips used for barbecuing) in water overnight. This prevents them from burning. The chips smolder, producing smoke that flavors the meat during the cooking process. The smoke also lends a pink color to the outer inch or so of the flesh, creating what is called a "smoke ring." A handful of wood chips should be added to the fire every 30 minutes or so. The more you add, the stronger flavor of smoke you get.

Place meat on the smoker or grill fat side down. After two hours, turn the meat over so it is fat side up. Total cook time will be $1\frac{1}{2}$ hours per pound. Maintain the temperature in the smoker between 225° and 250°. Use a pit thermometer for an accurate reading. If the smoker temperature is hotter than 250°, the meat will cook too quickly; any lower than 225°, and the meat will not get done. Every time wood chips or charcoal is added, spritz the meat with apple juice from a spray bottle. This will add moisture and a fruity background flavor during cooking.

Remove the meat from the smoker with two hours remaining, and place on heavy-duty aluminum foil. Spritz generously with apple juice, and tightly seal foil around pork. Place meat back on the smoker, and cook for two hours more. Using an instant-read meat thermometer, check the internal temperature of the thickest part of the meat, being careful not to touch bone with the tip of the thermometer. When the internal temperature reaches 195°, the pork is ready. Cooking the meat beyond the USDA guideline of 160° renders out the fat and tenderizes the meat.

Remove the meat from the smoker, and let it cool for 15 to 30 minutes. Remove foil after it has cooled enough to handle. Remove the bones, which will easily pull away. Begin pulling, or shredding, the meat with two large forks, and place in a large baking dish or pan. Remove and discard any remaining fat.

Add the sauce to pulled pork, and toss. This is a popular way to serve pulled pork in most regions. If you prefer, serve with additional sauce.

LOW COUNTRY BOIL

YIELD: *1 serving*

Donnie Walden
Powder Springs, Georgia

1/2	pound kielbasa
1/2	pound raw Georgia shrimp in shell, deveined
3	small new potatoes, scrubbed
1	ear corn, shucked
2	small onions
1	carrot, quartered
	Seasoning to taste (recommendations: 1/4 teaspoon cayenne, 1 teaspoon whole cloves, 1 clove garlic, 1 bay leaf, 1 tablespoon seafood seasoning, 1/2 teaspoon black pepper, 1/4 teaspoon hot sauce)
	Juice of 1/2 lemon or 1-2 tablespoons vinegar

Boil 1 quart water per serving in a large pot. Season the water with spices and lemon juice or vinegar. Add potatoes, carrots, sausage and onions. Bring back to a boil; cook until potatoes are almost tender. Add corn; boil for 5 minutes. Add shrimp and cook until shrimp are pink. Drain immediately.

Serve on a large platter accompanied by cocktail sauce, mustard, cornbread, cole slaw and watermelon.

MARINATED PORK LOIN WITH HOLIDAY SAUCE   (PICTURED ON PAGE 43)

YIELD: *10 servings*

1	cup low-sodium soy sauce
2	tablespoons lemon juice
1	tablespoon finely chopped garlic
2	tablespoons dried tarragon
2	tablespoons dried basil
1	3- to 4-pound boneless pork loin roast
	Holiday Sauce

Combine soy sauce, lemon juice, garlic and herbs in a small bowl; mix well. Place pork roast in heavy-duty plastic bag. Pour marinade mixture over pork. Marinate in refrigerator 5 hours or overnight.

Preheat oven to 325°.

Remove pork from marinade; reserve marinade. Place pork on rack in shallow roasting pan. Insert bulb of meat thermometer in thickest part of roast, away from fat. Roast 2 to 3 hours or until meat thermometer registers 160° for medium well or 170° for well done. Baste with marinade every 30 minutes. Remove from oven and let stand 15 minutes before slicing. Serve with Holiday Sauce.

Holiday Sauce

YIELD: *1 ½ cups*

1	12-ounce jar Georgia peach preserves
1	10-ounce jar apple jelly
4	tablespoons Dijon mustard
1	tablespoon prepared horseradish

Mix all ingredients. Cover and refrigerate. Serve with Marinated Pork Loin.

Try this marinade on pork tenderloin and cook either in the oven or on a grill.

Refrigerate leftover Holiday Sauce for spreading on leftover baked ham sandwiches.

These freeze well.

Children get a kick out of miniature things, which makes these Mini Meat Loaves just right for little hands in the kitchen. Try making this recipe when your grandchildren are visiting and you'll be amazed how proud kids can be of their own creation.

MINI MEAT LOAVES

Christine Northcutt
Jonesboro, Georgia

YIELD: *6 servings*

1	pound ground sirloin
1/2	cup chopped onion
1/2	cup chopped green pepper
1/2	cup chopped celery
1/2	cup dry breadcrumbs
1	egg, lightly beaten
1/2	cup milk
1/2	teaspoon salt
1/4	teaspoon ground black pepper
1/2	cup salsa
1	cup barbecue sauce

Preheat oven to 400°.

Combine all ingredients except salsa and barbecue sauce in large bowl; mix well. Set aside.

Combine salsa and barbecue sauce; reserve half of the mixture for topping. Add half of the sauce mixture to the meat mixture.

Lightly grease a 12-cup muffin tin. Spoon approximately 1/2 cup of the mixture into each muffin cup. Spoon remaining sauce over top of each meat loaf. Bake for 18 to 20 minutes.

Crushed corn flake crumbs will give a golden color to the coating.

Use chicken tenders and reduce cooking time to 20 minutes.

OVEN-FRIED CHICKEN

YIELD: *4 servings*

1	cup finely crushed cracker crumbs
2	teaspoons paprika
2	teaspoons salt
1/4	teaspoon pepper
1/4	cup butter, melted
1	2- to 3-pound broiler-fryer, cut up

Preheat oven to 350°.

Combine cracker crumbs, paprika, salt and pepper; mix well. Dip chicken in melted butter, dredge in crumb mixture and place in a lightly greased 13x9-inch baking dish.

Bake for 1 hour and 10 minutes.

Peach Glazed Chicken

Yield: *4 servings*

	Cooking spray
1	teaspoon vegetable oil
1	pound chicken breast tenders
½	cup Georgia peach preserves
2	tablespoons balsamic vinegar
1	green onion, chopped
¼	teaspoon pepper

Coat a large nonstick skillet with cooking spray; add oil, and place over medium high heat until hot. Add chicken and sauté 5 minutes on each side or until done. Remove chicken; set aside, and keep warm.

Reduce heat to low; add preserves then remaining 3 ingredients. Cook, stirring constantly, until preserves melt and onion is tender. Spoon mixture over chicken.

Pecan Trout

Georgia Pecan Commission

Yield: *4 servings*

4	rainbow trout fillets
½	cup all-purpose flour
2	tablespoons butter
⅓	cup butter
⅓	cup chopped Georgia pecans
2	teaspoons chopped green onion
1	teaspoon lemon juice

Lightly flour fillets. Melt 2 tablespoons butter in large skillet over medium heat. Pan fry fillets 2 minutes on one side and 1 minute on other. Remove fish from pan and keep warm.

Melt ⅓ cup butter in small saucepan over low heat and add remaining ingredients. Stir until well combined; spoon sauce over trout.

Have you ever caught trout? Share a fishing story here and tell what you remember the most about that adventure.

PORK CHOPS WITH GLAZED APPLE AND ONION

YIELD: *4 servings*

4	center cut boneless pork chops, $^3/_4$-inch thick
1	teaspoon vegetable oil
1	medium onion, thinly sliced
1	large Georgia apple, sliced
$^1/_2$	cup honey mustard
$^1/_4$	cup apple juice

Brown pork chops in oil in large skillet over medium-high heat. Reduce heat to medium; cook 5 to 10 minutes or until chops are done. Remove to serving platter and set aside.

Cook onion in pan drippings in same skillet over medium-high heat for 3 minutes, stirring occasionally. Add apple; cook 5 minutes or until apple and onion are tender. Stir in mustard and juice; heat through. Spoon sauce over chops.

"A family favorite passed down from the Iowa Farmer Today."

— *Paulette Korn*

QUICK LASAGNA

YIELD: *8 servings*

Paulette Korn
Dallas, Georgia

1	pound ground beef, browned and drained
9	lasagna noodles, cooked
1	26-ounce jar spaghetti sauce
1	8-ounce can tomato sauce
1	12-ounce carton cottage cheese
16	ounces mozzarella cheese, grated
$^1/_4$	cup grated Parmesan cheese

Preheat oven to 350°.

Combine spaghetti sauce and tomato sauce in a medium mixing bowl; set aside.

Place a small amount of sauce mixture in a greased 13x9-inch baking pan. Top with 3 lasagna noodles. Spread with $^1/_3$ of the sauce, ground beef, cottage cheese and mozzarella. Repeat layering twice. Sprinkle with Parmesan cheese. Cover and bake for 20 minutes.

Remove from oven; uncover and let stand for 10 minutes before slicing.

ROASTED PORK WITH FALL VEGETABLES

YIELD: *8 servings*

2	small onions, peeled and quartered
1	tablespoon olive oil, divided
1	cup cubed and peeled rutabaga
1	cup cubed and peeled turnips
2	cups cubed sweet potatoes
1	16-ounce package baby carrots
1	2 1/2-pound boneless pork loin roast
2	tablespoons chopped fresh sage
1	teaspoon salt, divided
1	teaspoon pepper
1	cup chicken broth
1/2	cup dry white wine, optional
1	tablespoon Dijon mustard

Preheat oven to 400°.

Heat 1 1/2 teaspoons oil in a large non-stick skillet over medium-high heat. Add onion; sauté 8 minutes or until lightly browned, stirring frequently. Remove onion from pan. Add remaining oil and vegetables to pan. Sauté 5 minutes or until lightly browned, stirring frequently.

Place pork roast on rack coated with cooking spray; place rack in shallow roasting pan. Sprinkle roast with sage, 1/2 teaspoon each salt and pepper. Arrange vegetables around roast; sprinkle vegetables with remaining salt and pepper.

Bake for 50 minutes or until meat thermometer registers 160°. Remove pork and vegetables from pan. Place pan over medium heat; stir in broth, wine and mustard, scraping pan to loosen browned bits. Bring to a boil; reduce heat and simmer 4 minutes, stirring occasionally. Serve with pork and vegetables.

SANTA FE CHICKEN AND RICE

Ester Case
Dawsonville, Georgia

YIELD: *6 servings*

1	tablespoon olive oil
2	tablespoons melted margarine
1 ½	cups rice
1	medium onion, chopped
3	cloves garlic, minced
1	16-ounce jar picante sauce
6	boneless, skinless chicken breast halves
1	14.5-ounce can chicken broth
1	cup shredded mozzarella cheese
1	medium tomato, chopped
	Parsley flakes

Preheat oven to 350°.

Combine olive oil and margarine in a 13x9-inch baking dish. Mix in rice, onions and garlic. Bake until lightly browned (about 15 minutes). Stir in picante sauce. Place chicken breasts over rice mixture. Pour chicken broth over chicken and rice. Cover tightly with foil and bake for 45 to 55 minutes.

Remove from oven; remove foil and cover chicken with shredded cheese and tomatoes. Return to oven to melt cheese. Sprinkle with parsley flakes.

SHRIMP AND CRAB CASSEROLE

YIELD: *6 servings*

Ricky Boone
*McIntosh County,
Georgia*

Treat yourself! Don't think of this recipe as a company-only dish. It's easy to prepare and very tasty.

1	medium green pepper, chopped
1	medium onion, chopped
1	pound lump crabmeat
1	pound Georgia shrimp, cleaned and cooked
½	teaspoon salt
¼	teaspoon pepper
1	teaspoon Worcestershire sauce
1	cup mayonnaise
1	cup crushed potato chips

Preheat oven to 350°.

Combine all ingredients except potato chips in large mixing bowl; stir to mix. Pour into lightly greased 2-quart baking dish. Top with crushed potato chips. Bake for 30 minutes.

Gay Jacobs
McIntosh County, Georgia

Gay Jacobs' advice on cooking shrimp: "The only way you can ruin shrimp is to overcook them."

SHRIMP AND PASTA, RICE OR GRITS

YIELD: *6 generous servings*

3	tablespoons olive oil
3	cloves garlic, chopped
1	cup coarsely chopped onion
1	roasted red sweet pepper, chopped
1/4	cup butter
1/2	cup all-purpose flour
1 1/2	teaspoons salt
1/2	teaspoon pepper
1/2	teaspoon lemon pepper
1/2	teaspoon seasoned salt
2-3	cups water
3	tablespoons tomato paste
2	pounds Georgia shrimp, peeled and deveined
1	teaspoon Worcestershire sauce
1/4	cup sherry, optional
3	tablespoons capers
	Cooked pasta, rice or grits

Sauté garlic, onion and red pepper in olive oil until crisp-tender; remove from pan and set aside.

Add butter, flour and dry ingredients; cook until golden brown, making a roux. Stir until smooth; add water gradually, stirring to prevent lumps. When gravy begins to thicken, add tomato paste. Bring mixture to a boil; add shrimp and continue cooking, stirring occasionally, until shrimp are pink (no more than 5 minutes). Stir in reserved onion mixture, Worcestershire sauce, sherry and capers. Remove from heat and serve immediately over pasta, rice or grits.

Shrimp Creole

Yield: *12 to 15 servings*

Ester Case
Dawsonville, Georgia

It will take about 30 minutes to make the roux. Don't get in a hurry or the mixture will burn and you'll have to start over!

1	cup cooking oil
1	cup all-purpose flour
1	large onion, chopped
1	medium green pepper, chopped
2	4-ounce cans tomato sauce
	Red pepper and salt to taste
2-3	cups water
2	quarts Georgia shrimp, peeled and deveined
	Dried Parsley or chopped green onion
	Hot sauce sauce, optional
	Hot cooked rice

Make a roux by combining cooking oil and flour in large heavy saucepan. Cook over medium heat until the mixture is brown or, as some say, "the color of a copper penny."

Add onion and green pepper. Sauté until vegetables are limp. Add tomato sauce, seasonings and enough water to keep it from being too thick but not gumbo watery, approximately 2 to 3 cups. Cook slowly until vegetables are done (about 45 minutes). Stir occasionally to prevent sticking.

Add shrimp and cook until shrimp turn pink, about 5 minutes. (If using frozen shrimp, thaw first under cold running water.)

Add parsley or chopped green onion just before serving. Serve over hot cooked rice.

This shredded beef is fitting for any occasion, but it is especially popular when taken to covered dish suppers.

SLOW-COOKER BARBECUED BEEF

YIELD: *12 servings*

1	3 ½-pound eye-of-round roast, cut in half vertically
2	teaspoons salt, divided
2	cloves garlic, minced
1	10-ounce can condensed beef broth
1	cup ketchup
½	cup firmly packed light brown sugar
½	cup lemon juice
3	tablespoons steak sauce
1	teaspoon pepper
1	teaspoon Worcestershire sauce
	Sandwich buns or rolls

Sprinkle beef evenly with 1 teaspoon salt. Stir together remaining ingredients. Pour half of mixture in slow cooker. Place beef in pot, and pour remaining mixture over beef. Cover and cook on HIGH 7 hours. Shred beef in slow cooker with two forks. Serve on rolls or buns.

SOUTHERN SHEPHERD'S PIE WITH CORNBREAD TOPPING

Reba Hightower
Flowery Branch, Georgia

YIELD: *6 servings*

2	pounds lean ground beef round
	Salt to taste
1	8-ounce can mushroom stems and pieces, drained
1	1-pound 10-ounce jar chunky-style pasta sauce
	Cornbread Topping

Preheat oven to 400°.

Brown ground round, drain liquid. Salt to taste; add drained mushrooms and pasta sauce. Pour into 2-quart baking dish (deep and narrow shape works best).

Top with thin crust of Cornbread Topping. Bake for 30 minutes or until topping is brown.

Cornbread Topping

1	cup buttermilk self-rising cornmeal mix
1	egg, lightly beaten
¼	cup vegetable oil
¾	cup buttermilk

Combine all ingredients in small bowl. Stir until moistened. Batter will be thin. Spread evenly over meat mixture. Bake as directed above.

For additional color and taste, 1 cup frozen peas or green beans could be added to the mixture.

Diane Pendley
Oakwood, Georgia

SWEET AND SOUR MEATBALLS

YIELD: *4 to 6 servings*

1	pound ground beef
1	cup milk
1	teaspoon salt
½	teaspoon ground black pepper
½	cup cracker crumbs
1	medium green pepper, chopped
1	cup chopped onion
1	cup ketchup
3	tablespoons Worcestershire sauce
½	cup sugar
½	cup cider vinegar

Preheat oven to 350°.

Combine ground beef, milk, salt, pepper and cracker crumbs in a large mixing bowl; mix thoroughly. Shape into 10 large meatballs. Place in a single layer in an 8-inch baking dish.

Combine remaining ingredients. Pour sauce mixture over meat balls. Bake for 1 hour. (If sauce cooks down too fast, cover baking pan with foil.)

These freeze well and can be made into a smaller size for snacks.

To shape meatballs quickly, pat the meat mixture out into a square of consistent thickness. Cut into equal portions/squares with a large knife and shape into balls with your hands.

DESSERTS

It's no secret that we Southerners appreciate living life at a relaxed pace. We take pleasure in sunsets over the farm, a well-told story, gentle breezes, and yes, we like our sweets. Whether baked, fried, frozen or frosted, desserts are a constant in Southern life.

This Desserts section will introduce you to Apple Rollups *(pg. 150)* and Low Sugar Pumpkin Pie *(pg. 171)* as well as reacquaint you with popular desserts of the past, including Chocolate Sundae Pudding *(pg. 160)* and Luscious Lemon Squares *(pg. 172)*.

Thanks to Georgia farmers, we are able to enjoy Individual Peach Cheesecakes *(pg. 170)*, Sweet Potato Pie with Praline Topping *(pg. 180)*, and Pecan Kiss Cakes *(pg. 175)*. No one can argue that desserts make life in Georgia that much sweeter.

Filled with fruit and nuts and crisp when first baked, these become moist after being stored for a few days.

Need to take a home-made treat to a baby shower, brunch or tea party? These fruity goodies can be made in advance, placed in air-tight containers and gifted with or without a ribbon.

AMBROSIA COOKIES

Mrs. Ray Oakes
LaGrange, Georgia

YIELD: *4 dozen*

1	cup butter
1	cup sugar
1	cup firmly packed light brown sugar
2	eggs, well beaten
1	teaspoon vanilla extract
2	cups all-purpose flour
1	teaspoon baking powder
½	teaspoon baking soda
¼	teaspoon salt
1	cup flaked coconut
1 ½	cups uncooked quick-cooking oats
1	cup chopped Georgia pecans
2	cups raisins or chopped dates (or 1 cup each)
1	tablespoon grated lemon rind
1	tablespoon grated orange rind

Preheat oven to 375°.

Cream butter and sugars in a large mixing bowl. Add eggs, beating well; stir in vanilla. Set aside.

Combine flour with remaining ingredients in a medium mixing bowl. Add to creamed mixture, stirring well. Drop by teaspoonfuls onto ungreased cookie sheets. Bake for 10 to 12 minutes. Remove to wire racks to cool.

Store in airtight containers.

APPLE FRITTERS

YIELD: *6 servings*

Kyla Hall
Unadilla, Georgia

3   cups peeled and chopped Georgia apples
1   cup all-purpose flour
1   teaspoon baking powder
¼   teaspoon salt
2   teaspoons powdered sugar
1   egg, beaten
¼   cup milk
       Vegetable oil for deep frying
       Powdered sugar for dusting

Peel and chop apples; set aside.

Combine flour, baking powder, salt, 2 teaspoons powdered sugar, egg and milk in a large mixing bowl. Stir to moisten. Add apples and mix well.

Drop by teaspoons into hot oil. Fry until golden brown; drain on paper towels. Sprinkle with additional powdered sugar. Serve hot.

Pears can be substituted for apples.

These are delicious served with maple syrup.

These taste similar to apple dumplings but are quicker and easier to make.

They are also delicious for breakfast — without the ice cream.

APPLE ROLLUPS

Marie Couch
Dallas, Georgia

YIELD: *8 rollups*

1	8-ounce package refrigerated crescent rolls
2	Georgia apples, peeled, cored and cut into eighths
1/2	cup sugar
1/2	teaspoon ground cinnamon
1/8	teaspoon ground allspice
1/2	cup water
2	tablespoons butter or margarine
	Vanilla ice cream, optional

Preheat oven to 400°,

Separate crescent rolls into 4 rectangles; roll to 1/8-inch thickness on a lightly floured surface. Cut each rectangle into 4 strips. Place one apple wedge on each strip, roll up tightly and place, seam side down, in a 10x6-inch baking dish.

Combine sugar, cinnamon and allspice; sprinkle over apple rollups. Pour water over rollups and dot with butter. Bake for 20 minutes or until lightly browned. Serve hot with ice cream.

Apricot-Oatmeal Bars

Yield: *about 2 dozen bars*

Mrs. Bettie Evans
Kennesaw, Georgia

1 ½	cups all-purpose flour
1 ½	cups uncooked quick-cooking oats
½	cup sugar
½	teaspoon baking soda
¼	teaspoon salt
¾	cup softened butter or margarine
2	teaspoons vanilla extract
1	10-ounce jar apricot preserves
½	cup flaked coconut

Preheat oven to at 350˚.

Combine first 5 ingredients in a large mixing bowl. Blend well. Add butter and vanilla; mix until mixture is crumbly. Set aside 1 cup mixture.

Press remaining crumb mixture into a greased 13x9-inch baking pan. Spread apricot preserves over crust to within ½ inch of edge of pan.

Sprinkle with reserved crumb mixture and coconut. Bake for 25 to 30 minutes or until light brown. Cool and cut into bars.

These are a hit with a glass of cold milk.

For variety, try making these bars with raspberry jam or preserves.

Use this page as a cross reference to your favorite cookies. Did someone special teach you how to bake them?

The Lemon Sauce is delicious and would be good on pound cake or warm gingerbread.

BREAD PUDDING WITH LEMON SAUCE

Sara T. Dukes
Bartow, Georgia

YIELD: *6 to 8 servings*

3	eggs
1	cup sugar
3	cups bread cubes
1 ¾	cup milk, warmed
2	tablespoons melted butter
½	teaspoon ground cinnamon
½	teaspoon ground nutmeg
½	teaspoon vanilla extract
½	cup raisins
	Dash salt
	Lemon Sauce

Preheat oven to 350°.

Beat eggs and sugar in large mixing bowl. Add remaining ingredients except Lemon Sauce, stirring to combine. Pour into a greased 2-quart baking dish. Bake for 50 minutes or until center is set. Cut into squares and serve warm with Lemon Sauce.

Lemon Sauce

YIELD: *approximately 1 cup*

1	egg, beaten
1	cup sugar
	Grated rind of 1 lemon
	Juice of 2 lemons
1	tablespoon butter

Combine sugar, egg, lemon juice and rind. Cook over medium heat stirring constantly, until thick (about 5 minutes after it starts boiling). Stir in butter to melt.

Cook over low heat, stirring constantly, until mixture thickens. Serve warm.

Brown Sugar Pound Cake with Buttermilk Glaze

Marie Couch
Dallas, Georgia

YIELD: *1 (10-inch) cake*

2	sticks butter, softened
2	cups firmly packed light brown sugar
1	cup granulated sugar
6	eggs
3	cups sifted all-purpose flour
1/2	teaspoon salt
1/2	teaspoon baking powder
1	cup milk
1	teaspoon vanilla extract
1	teaspoon maple extract
	Buttermilk Glaze, optional

Preheat oven to 350°.

Beat butter and sugars at medium speed of electric mixer until light and fluffy. Add eggs, beating well after each addition.

Combine dry ingredients; add to butter mixture alternately with milk, beginning and ending with flour mixture. Stir in flavorings.

Pour batter into a greased and floured 10-inch tube pan. Bake for 1 1/4 hours or until a wooden pick inserted in center comes out clean. Cool in pan on wire rack 10 minutes; remove from pan, and cool completely on wire rack.

Place on serving plate. If desired, pour warm Buttermilk Glaze over cake.

Buttermilk Glaze

1	cup sugar
1 1/2	teaspoons baking soda
1/2	cup buttermilk
1/2	cup butter
1	tablespoon light corn syrup
1	teaspoon vanilla extract

Bring first 5 ingredients to a boil in large Dutch oven over medium heat. Boil 4 minutes, stirring constantly until glaze is golden. Remove from heat, and stir in vanilla. Cool slightly.

Testing with a knife will cause the cheesecake to crack in the center. Use either a cake tester or toothpick.

When cheesecake is cooling on the rack, run a knife around the edges to loosen. This will also prevent cracking.

CHEESECAKE (PICTURED ON PAGE 48)

Emma Smith
Grayson, Georgia

YIELD: *1 (9-inch) cake*

1 ½	cups finely rolled graham cracker crumbs
¼	cup sugar
¼	cup butter, softened
3	8-ounce packages cream cheese
6	eggs
1	cup sugar
1	teaspoon vanilla extract
1	16-ounce container sour cream
5	tablespoons sugar
1	teaspoon vanilla extract

Preheat oven to 300°.

Combine graham cracker crumbs, ¼ cup sugar and butter in a small bowl. Stir to combine. (Coat sides of pan lightly with butter to hold crumbs in place.) Press crumb mixture firmly onto bottom and sides of a 9-inch spring form pan. Set aside.

Beat cream cheese at medium speed with electric mixer until smooth and creamy. Add eggs, one at a time, beating well after each addition. Gradually add sugar, beating well. Add vanilla; beat well. Pour carefully into prepared crust. Bake for 1 hour 15 minutes or until cake tester inserted in center comes out clean. Remove from oven for 10 minutes.

Combine sour cream, sugar and vanilla. Spread over cheesecake. Return to oven. Bake for 5 minutes. Remove from oven and place on wire rack to cool completely. Cover and chill 8 hours.

Toasting pecans enhances their flavor.

CHERRY FLUFF

Minnie L. Tiller
Athens, Georgia

YIELD: *12 to 16 servings*

1	8-ounce carton frozen whipped topping, thawed
1	20-ounce can crushed pineapple, drained
1	21-ounce can cherry pie filling
1	14-ounce can sweetened condensed milk
½	cup flaked coconut
½	cup chopped Georgia pecans

Combine all ingredients in a large bowl; stir to mix well. Chill overnight.

CHOCOLATE CHIP PECAN PIE

Lauren McMann
Blairsville, Georgia

YIELD: *1 (9-inch) pie*

1	stick butter, softened
1	cup sugar
½	cup self-rising flour
2	eggs, lightly beaten
1	tablespoon vanilla extract
1	cup chopped Georgia pecans
1	cup semi-sweet chocolate chips
1	unbaked 9-inch pie crust
	Ice cream or whipped cream, optional

Preheat oven to 325°.

Combine butter, sugar, flour and eggs in a large mixing bowl. Stir to combine.

Mix in next 3 ingredients. Pour mixture into unbaked pie crust.

Bake for 50 minutes. Remove from oven and cool to room temperature. Serve with ice cream or whipped cream, if desired.

CHOCOLATE CHIP TOFFEE BARS

Nancy Reeves
Smyrna, Georgia

YIELD: *about 2 dozen*

11	whole graham crackers, broken into squares
1	cup butter
1	cup sugar
1	teaspoon ground cinnamon
½	cup finely chopped and toasted Georgia pecans
1	6-ounce package semisweet chocolate mini-chips

Preheat oven to 350°.

Arrange graham crackers in single layer in a 15x10x1-inch jelly roll pan. Set aside.

Combine butter and sugar in a medium saucepan. Cook over medium heat, stirring until butter melts. Bring to a boil; boil 2 minutes. Remove from heat; stir in cinnamon and pecans. Pour over graham crackers, spreading evenly to edges of pan.

Bake for 10 minutes. Sprinkle with chocolate chips. Cool 5 minutes; separate cookies and transfer to waxed paper-lined cookie sheets, using a spatula. Refrigerate until chocolate hardens. Store cookies between layers of waxed paper in an airtight container in the refrigerator.

"These bars don't take many ingredients or much time, but are always a favorite at family gatherings."
— *Nancy Reeves*

These must be chilled and handled carefully, but they taste great! They are a cross between a cookie and candy.

CHOCOLATE ITALIAN CREAM CAKE WITH CHOCOLATE CREAM CHEESE FROSTING

Imogene Porter
Buford, Georgia

YIELD: *1 3-layer (8-inch) cake*

½	cup softened butter
½	cup shortening
2	cups sugar
5	eggs, separated
1	teaspoon baking soda
2	cups sifted all-purpose flour
¼	cup unsweetened cocoa
1	cup buttermilk
1	cup flaked coconut
1	teaspoon vanilla extract
½ - 1	cup chopped Georgia pecans
	Chocolate Cream Cheese Frosting

Preheat oven to 325°.

Grease and flour three 8-inch cake pans; set aside.

Beat butter and shortening at medium speed with an electric mixer until creamy; gradually add sugar, beating until light and fluffy. Add egg yolks one at a time, beating well after each addition.

Sift baking soda, flour and cocoa. Add to butter mixture alternately with buttermilk, beginning and ending with dry ingredients. Stir in coconut, vanilla and nuts. Set aside.

Beat egg whites in a large mixing bowl at high speed until stiff peaks form. Fold into batter.

Pour batter into prepared pans. Bake for 25 to 30 minutes or until wooden pick inserted in center comes out clean. Cool in pan on wire rack.

When completely cooled, frost with Chocolate Cream Cheese Frosting (next page).

Chocolate Cream Cheese Frosting

1	8-ounce package cream cheese, softened
$\frac{1}{2}$	cup butter, softened
1	teaspoon vanilla extract
1	1-pound package powdered sugar
$\frac{1}{4}$	cup unsweetened cocoa
$\frac{1}{2}$ – 1	cup chopped Georgia pecans
	Georgia pecan halves for garnish

Beat softened cream cheese and butter at medium speed with an electric mixer until smooth.

Sift powdered sugar and cocoa. Gradually add to creamed mixture with vanilla extract, beating at low speed until light and fluffy. Stir in $\frac{1}{2}$ to 1 cup chopped pecans.

Spread a thin layer of frosting on tops of completely cooled layers. Stack layers and frost sides of cake. Garnish with pecan halves.

Special requests? Do you have family members who request specific cakes for birthdays or other celebrations? List your family's favorite cakes and share a story about why they like them.

CHOCOLATE RASPBERRY CAKE

YIELD: *1 (13x9-inch) cake*

Rebecca Short
Dahlonega, Georgia

1	19.5-ounce package dark chocolate cake mix
3	eggs
1/3	cup vegetable oil
1	3-ounce package raspberry flavor gelatin
1	cup boiling water
1	14-ounce can sweetened condensed milk
1	10-ounce jar seedless raspberry jam
1	8-ounce carton frozen whipped topping, thawed

Prepare cake mix according to package directions using 3 eggs and 1/3 cup oil.

Bake in a 13x9-inch pan for shortest time recommended.

While cake bakes, dissolve gelatin in boiling water. Remove cake from oven and immediately punch holes in cake with handle of wooden spoon. Pour gelatin over hot cake. Pour sweetened condensed milk over cake. Spread raspberry jam over cake.

Refrigerate overnight. Remove from refrigerator and spread with whipped topping.

Store cake in refrigerator.

CHOCOLATE SHEET CAKE WITH CHOCOLATE FROSTING

YIELD: *1 (13x9-inch) cake*

2	cups all-purpose flour
2	cups sugar
1/4	cup unsweetened cocoa
1	teaspoon ground cinnamon
1	cup butter or margarine
1	cup water
1	teaspoon baking soda
2	large eggs
1/2	cup buttermilk
1	teaspoon vanilla
	Chocolate Frosting

Preheat oven to 350°.

Combine first 4 ingredients in a large mixing bowl and set aside.

Combine butter and water in a saucepan and bring to a boil.

Remove from heat; stir in baking soda. Pour hot mixture over dry ingredients, stirring well with a wooden spoon. Stir in eggs, buttermilk and vanilla.

Pour batter into a greased and floured 13x9-inch pan. Bake for 30 minutes. While cake is baking, prepare the Chocolate Frosting. Remove cake from oven and immediately pour on frosting.

Chocolate Frosting

1/2	cup butter or margarine
1/3	cup milk
1	1-pound box powdered sugar, sifted
1/4	cup unsweetened cocoa
1	teaspoon vanilla extract

Combine butter and milk in a large saucepan. Bring to a boil; remove from heat and stir in powdered sugar and cocoa. Add vanilla. Pour over hot cake.

Dress up this traditional cake with a sprinkling of chopped, toasted Georgia pecans over the frosting.

CHOCOLATE SNICKER PIE

YIELD: *6 or 8 servings*

Lila F. Weatherly
Dublin, Georgia

2	cups softened low-fat chocolate frozen yogurt
1/3	cup reduced fat crunchy peanut butter
1/2	cup grape nuts cereal
1	8-ounce container fat-free frozen whipped topping, thawed

Combine all ingredients in a large mixing bowl. Spoon mixture into a 9-inch glass pie plate or 9-inch square baking dish. Place in freezer for several hours or overnight. Remove from freezer 10 minutes before serving. Cut into wedges to serve.

CHOCOLATE SUNDAE PUDDING

YIELD: *6 servings*

Sue Lamb
Vidalia, Georgia

1	cup all-purpose flour
2	teaspoons baking powder
1/2	teaspoon salt
3/4	cup sugar
1	egg, beaten
1/2	cup milk
2	tablespoons melted shortening
1	cup chopped Georgia pecans
6	tablespoons unsweetened cocoa
1	cup firmly packed light brown sugar
1 3/4	cup hot water
	Whipped cream, optional

Preheat oven to 350°.

Sift together first 4 ingredients in a large mixing bowl. Add egg, milk and shortening; mix until smooth. Stir in pecans. Spread mixture in a 9x9-inch baking pan.

Combine cocoa and brown sugar in a small bowl. Sprinkle over the batter. Pour hot water into a tablespoon and let flow over sugar mixture.

Bake for 45 minutes. Serve warm with whipped cream, if desired.

CRANBERRY APPLE CRUMBLE WITH CRUMB TOPPING

Helga Darty
Ellenwood, Georgia

YIELD: *8 servings*

½	cup all-purpose flour
½	cup sugar
½	cup firmly packed light brown sugar
½	teaspoon ground cinnamon
¼ - ½	teaspoon ground nutmeg
4	cups peeled, cored and thinly sliced Georgia apples
2	cups fresh or frozen whole cranberries
¼	cup water
	Crumb Topping
	Vanilla ice cream, optional

Peheat oven to 400.°

Combine flour, sugars, cinnamon and nutmeg in a large bowl. Add apples and cranberries; toss to coat with flour mixture. Place in 2 quart casserole. Pour water over fruit mixture. Sprinkle with Crumb Topping. Bake for 40 to 45 minutes.

Serve warm with ice cream!

Crumb Topping

⅔	cup all-purpose flour
½	cup sugar
½	cup butter

Stir together flour and sugar in medium bowl. Cut in butter until mixture is crumbly. Sprinkle over fruit mixture.

CREAMY CANTALOUPE POPS

Runette Bell
Jeffersonville, Georgia

YIELD: *8 servings*

1 ½	cups cubed ripe cantaloupe
1	cup heavy whipping cream
½	cup sugar
8	ice pop molds with sticks

Place cantaloupe in blender or food processor and process until smooth. Set aside.

In a small saucepan combine cream and sugar. Cook and stir over low heat until sugar dissolves. Remove from heat. Stir in puréed cantaloupe. Pour into ice pop molds. Insert sticks. Freeze until firm.

CRUNCHY APPLE CAKE

H. Mathis
Americus, Georgia

YIELD: *1 (8-inch) cake*

1	21-ounce can apple pie filling
1	stick butter, melted
1	small box white or yellow cake mix
1	cup chopped Georgia pecans

Preheat oven to 375°.

Spread pie filling in bottom of 8-inch square baking pan. Sprinkle dry cake mix over filling. Pour melted butter over cake mix; sprinkle nuts over butter.

Bake for 45 minutes or until top is brown and filling bubbles.

These would be great with ripe peaches, strawberries or other types of melon.

For a "grown-up" dessert, freeze in foil cupcake papers, remove foil and serve in small stemmed glasses with a shortbread cookie on the side.

Quick, easy and good! Serve warm topped with homemade-style vanilla ice cream.

If single layer cake mixes are not available, use half of a 19-ounce package or double the ingredients and bake in a 13x9-inch pan.

CRUNCHY CHOCOLATE GRAHAMS

C. Jay Spell, III
College Park, Georgia

These are really good, but the mixture does harden quickly!

YIELD: *2 dozen cookies*

	Cooking oil spray
2	individual packs honey graham crackers (about 24 crackers)
18	ounces milk chocolate chips
1	cup firmly packed light brown sugar
2	sticks margarine
½	cup chopped Georgia pecans

Preheat oven to 325°.

Lightly spray 2 large jelly roll pans (15x10-inch baking pans). Cover bottom of pans with one layer of graham crackers. Sprinkle chocolate chips over crackers. Set aside.

Combine sugar and margarine in a small saucepan; bring to a boil and cook 2½ minutes. Stir in pecans; boil another 30 seconds.

Drizzle sugar mixture over chocolate chips and graham crackers. Work quickly as mixture hardens as it cools. Spread evenly with back of spoon.

Bake for 10 to 12 minutes. Do not over bake; watch carefully as they burn easily. Cool completely; break into pieces. Store in airtight container.

DOUBLE CHOCOLATE BROWNIES (PICTURED ON PAGE 35)

YIELD: *24 brownies*

For easy removal of brownies or any bar cookie, line the baking pan with foil or parchment paper. Extend paper over ends of pan. When cool, lift cookies from pan by paper handles and cut into squares.

4	1-ounce squares unsweetened chocolate
¾	cup butter or margarine
2	cups sugar
3	eggs
½	cup milk
1	teaspoon vanilla extract
1½	cup all-purpose flour
1	cup coarsely chopped Georgia pecans
1	cup semi-sweet chocolate morsels

Preheat oven to 350°.

Combine chocolate and margarine in a large glass mixing bowl. Microwave on HIGH for 2 minutes or until butter melts. Stir until chocolate melts. Stir in remaining ingredients.

Spoon batter into greased 13x9-inch baking pan. Bake for 30 to 35 minutes. Remove from oven and cool in pan. Cut into squares.

If figs are unavailable, you can substitute dates.

Fig Cake with Buttermilk Glaze

Louise Allison
Doraville, Georgia

Yield: *1 (13x9-inch) cake*

2	cups all-purpose flour
1 ½	cups sugar
1	teaspoon salt
1	teaspoon soda
1	teaspoon ground cloves
1	teaspoon ground nutmeg
1	teaspoon ground cinnamon
3	large eggs, lightly beaten
1	cup vegetable oil
1	cup buttermilk
1	teaspoon vanilla extract
1	cup chopped fresh figs or fig preserves (If using fresh figs, remove the stems!)
1	cup chopped Georgia pecans, optional
	Buttermilk Glaze

Preheat oven to 325°.

Sift together first 7 ingredients. Stir in eggs, oil and buttermilk, blending well.

Stir in vanilla; fold in figs and pecans. Pour into a greased and floured 13x9-inch pan. Bake at for 55 minutes or until a wooden pick inserted in center comes out clean. Pierce top of cake several times with wooden pick; pour Buttermilk Glaze over warm cake.

Buttermilk Glaze

1	cup sugar
½	cup buttermilk
1	teaspoon light corn syrup
1	teaspoon vanilla extract

Combine all ingredients in medium saucepan. Bring to a boil and cook 3 minutes. Remove from heat and pour over warm cake.

FLAG-WAVING PEANUT BUTTER COOKIES

YIELD: *4 dozen cookies*

National Peanut Board

½	cup softened butter
1	cup creamy peanut butter
½	cup granulated sugar
½	cup packed light brown sugar
½	teaspoon vanilla
1	egg
1 ½	cups all-purpose flour
¾	teaspoon baking soda
½	teaspoon baking powder
¼	teaspoon salt

Preheat oven to 350˚.

Combine first six ingredients. Beat until light and fluffy.

Stir the dry ingredients together and add to butter mixture. Blend thoroughly. Shape into 1-inch balls and place about 2 inches apart on ungreased baking sheet. Flatten with fork tines.

Bake for 10 minutes or until lightly browned.

Bake a batch of these all-American cookies for a July 4th cookout. Serve with homemade ice cream (pg. 168 and pg. 181) and watch the flags wave with excitement!

Chloe Petron
Taylorsville, Georgia

FRESH APPLE CAKE WITH CARAMEL TOPPING

YIELD: *1 (10-inch) cake*

Pears can be substituted for all or part of the apples.

Add one cup fresh chopped figs for a different taste.

The topping takes time but is worth it. It is thick and sweet and good enough to eat by itself!

2	cups sugar
1 1/2	cups vegetable oil
3	eggs
1	teaspoon vanilla
1/4	cup orange juice
3	cups all-purpose flour
1	teaspoon ground cinnamon
1	teaspoon baking soda
1/4	teaspoon salt
2	cups peeled and chopped Georgia apples
1	cup flaked coconut
1	cup chopped Georgia pecans
	Caramel Topping, optional

Preheat oven to 325°.

Combine sugar, oil, eggs, vanilla and orange juice in large mixing bowl. Mix at low speed of electric mixer until creamy.

Stir dry ingredients in a small bowl to combine. Add to creamed mixture and mix until dry ingredients are moistened. Stir in apples, coconut and pecans.

Pour into greased and floured 10-inch tube or Bundt pan. Bake for 1 hour or until wooden pick inserted in center comes out clean. Cool in pan on wire rack 10 minutes; remove from pan and cool completely on wire rack. Spoon Caramel Topping over the top and sides of warm cake, if desired.

Caramel Topping

1	cup sugar
1/2	teaspoon baking soda
1/2	cup butter
1/2	cup buttermilk

Combine all ingredients in medium saucepan. Bring to a boil; reduce heat to medium and cook for 20 minutes, stirring constantly. Remove from heat; beat until smooth.

GINGERBREAD MEN

YIELD: *about 3 dozen, depending on size of cookie cutters*

Betty Smith
Warner Robins, Georgia

1	cup shortening
1	cup firmly packed dark brown sugar
1	cup molasses
1	egg
4	cups all-purpose flour
1	teaspoon salt
1	teaspoon baking soda
2	teaspoons ground ginger
1	teaspoon ground cinnamon
1/2	teaspoon ground nutmeg
1/2	teaspoon ground cloves
	Raisins
	Red cinnamon candies
	Decorator Frosting

Preheat oven to 375°.

Cream shortening in large mixing bowl; gradually add brown sugar, beating until light and fluffy. Add molasses and egg; beat well.

Combine flour, salt, soda and spices; add to creamed mixture, blending well. Divide dough in half; chill 1 hour or until stiff enough to handle.

Roll one portion of dough to 1/4-inch thickness on lightly floured surface; cut into desired shapes. Place 2 inches apart on lightly greased cookie sheet. Press on raisins for eyes and cinnamon candies for buttons. Bake for 10 minutes. Remove to wire racks to cool. Decorate as desired with frosting.

"These are a holiday tradition in our family. We make all sizes and both men and women!"
—Betty Smith

These make the house smell wonderful while baking! The dough is easy to work with, re-rolls easily and added flour only makes crispier cookies.

For soft gingerbread men, roll thicker and bake only 8-10 minutes.

The crisp ones are good dunked in hot tea or cider.

HOMEMADE BLUEBERRY ICE CREAM   (PICTURED ON PAGE 30)

Georgia Fruit &
Vegetable Growers
Association

YIELD: *3 quarts*

3	cups fresh Georgia blueberries
½	cup water
2	pints half-and-half
1	quart milk
3	cups sugar

Crush blueberries; combine blueberries and water in large saucepan, bring to a boil over medium heat, stirring constantly. Remove from heat and strain to remove hulls. Pour remaining fruit into 1-gallon freezer container; add remaining ingredients, stirring to dissolve sugar. Freeze in an ice cream maker according to manufacturer's directions.

ICE CREAM SANDWICH DESSERT

Janie Foster
Cumming, Georgia

"Everyone always loves this dessert. It makes a lot and looks impressive!"

— *Janie Foster*

Kids and teens will enjoy assembling and devouring this frozen dessert.

YIELD: *18 servings*

1	16-ounce can chocolate syrup
¾	cup peanut butter
18	ice cream sandwiches
1	12-ounce container frozen whipped topping, thawed
1	cup salted Georgia peanuts

Place chocolate syrup in a medium mixing bowl. Microwave on HIGH for 2 minutes. Add peanut butter and stir until smooth. Set aside to cool to room temperature.

Line the bottom of a 13x9-inch pan with ice cream sandwiches. Spread half the whipped topping over the ice cream sandwiches. Spoon half the chocolate mixture over the whipped topping. Sprinkle with half the peanuts. Repeat layers.

Freeze 1 hour or until firm. Cut into squares to serve.

IMPOSSIBLE FRENCH APPLE PIE WITH STREUSEL TOPPING

YIELD: *1 (10-inch) pie*

Mrs. Burn
Savannah, Georgia

This pie is best served hot topped with vanilla bean ice cream.

6	cups peeled and sliced Georgia apples
1 1/4	teaspoon ground cinnamon
1/4	teaspoon ground nutmeg
1	cup sugar
1/2	cup biscuit baking mix
3/4	cup milk
2	eggs
2	tablespoons softened butter
	Streusel Topping
	Vanilla bean ice cream, optional

Preheat oven to 325°.

Combine apples, cinnamon and nutmeg in large mixing bowl. Pour into a greased 10-inch pie pan (or 9x9-inch baking dish). Combine remaining ingredients except Streusel Topping in large mixer bowl and mix until smooth. Pour over apples.

Sprinkle with Streusel Topping. Bake for 55 minutes. Serve warm with ice cream, if desired.

Streusel Topping

1	cup dry biscuit baking mix
1/3	cup firmly packed light brown sugar
1/3	cup butter
1/2	cup chopped Georgia pecans

Combine all ingredients in a small bowl. Mix with a fork until mixture is crumbly. Sprinkle over Impossible French Apple Pie before baking.

Thank the peach farmers for their contribution to this fabulous dessert. According to the Georgia Peach Commission, Georgia produces more than 130 million pounds of peaches annually, between mid-May and mid-August. More than 40 different varieties of peaches are grown in Georgia.

INDIVIDUAL PEACH CHEESECAKES (PICTURED ON PAGE 20)

YIELD: *12 servings*

Georgia Peach Commission

1	cup finely chopped Georgia pecans
2	tablespoons melted butter or margarine
1	envelope unflavored gelatin
1/4	cup cold water
2	8-ounce packages cream cheese, softened
1/2	cup sugar
3/4	cup skim milk
4	cups peeled and sliced Georgia peaches
	Fresh mint sprigs, optional

Combine pecans and butter in a small bowl. Spoon equal amounts of mixture into paper-lined muffin tins, pressing evenly.

Soften gelatin in cold water in a small saucepan; stir over low heat until dissolved. Set aside.

Combine softened cream cheese, sugar and milk in large bowl of electric mixer.

Beat at medium speed until well blended. Stir in gelatin. Pour into muffin tins; freeze until firm.

Purée 3 cups of the peaches in food processor or blender. Reserve 1 cup peach slices for garnish.

Remove cheesecakes from freezer 10 minutes before serving; peel off paper. Just before serving, spoon peach purée onto individual plates. Invert cheesecakes onto peach purée. Garnish with additional peach slices and fresh mint sprigs, if desired.

Lemon Chess Pie   (Pictured on page 26)

Mrs. Lois Knight
Jeffersonville, Georgia

YIELD: *1 (9-inch) pie*

1	9-inch unbaked pie crust
2	cups sugar
1	tablespoon all-purpose flour
1	tablespoon cornmeal
1/4	teaspoon salt
1/4	cup melted butter
1/4	cup fresh lemon juice
	Grated rind of 2 lemons
1/4	cup milk
4	eggs

Preheat oven to 350°.

Combine sugar, flour, cornmeal and salt in large mixing bowl. Add butter, lemon juice, lemon rind and milk. Mix well. Add eggs one at a time, beating well after each addition. Pour into unbaked pie crust.

Bake for 50 minutes or until knife inserted halfway between center and edge of pie comes out clean. Cool on rack.

Lemon Chess Pie is very rich and very Southern! Made from ingredients usually on hand, it is a simple yet elegant company dessert.

Low-Sugar Pumpkin Pie

Beverly Johnson
Conyers, Georgia

YIELD: *1 (9-inch) pie*

1	cup canned pumpkin
2	1-ounce packages sugar-free instant vanilla pudding
2	cups milk
1	teaspoon pumpkin pie spice
1	baked 9-inch pie crust or 1 6-ounce graham cracker crust

Combine pumpkin, pudding mix, milk and pumpkin pie spice in a large mixing bowl. Stir until mixture thickens, about 5 minutes. Pour into pie crust. Refrigerate until set.

Georgia Milk
Commission

*A 12-ounce jar of
lemon curd can be
substituted for the
lemon pudding layer.
Spread curd over cream
cheese layer and top
with whipped topping.*

LUSCIOUS LEMON SQUARES

YIELD: *10 to 12 servings*

½	cup butter
1	tablespoon sugar
1	cup flour
½	cup finely chopped Georgia pecans
1	cup powdered sugar
1	8-ounce package cream cheese, softened
1	12-ounce container frozen whipped topping, thawed
3	cups cold milk
1	6-ounce package package lemon instant pudding
2	tablespoons lemon juice
	Lemon slices, optional

Preheat oven to 350°.

Combine butter, sugar and flour in a small bowl; mix with a fork until crumbly.

Pat mixture into the bottom of a 13x9-inch baking pan. Bake for 15 to 20 minutes or until light brown. Set aside to cool.

Combine powdered sugar and cream cheese; mix at medium speed of electric mixer. Stir in 1 cup whipped topping; spread over crust. Set aside.

Combine milk, pudding mix and lemon juice in large mixing bowl. Stir until mixture thickens. Pour over cream cheese layer. Top with remaining whipped topping. Chill before serving. Garnish with lemon slices, if desired.

Orange Coconut Cake

YIELD: *1 2-layer (8-inch) cake*

Minnie L. Tiller
Athens, Georgia

This cake gets better as it stands.

It is delicious as an ice box cake, too!

1	18.25-ounce white cake mix
1	teaspoon orange extract
2	cups sugar
1	cup evaporated milk
2	tablespoons white corn syrup
2	tablespoons margarine or butter
1	cup orange juice
1	teaspoon orange extract
1	7-ounce package flaked coconut

Prepare cake mix according to package directions; stir in 1 teaspoon orange extract. Bake in 2 (8-inch) layers. Remove from the oven; cool completely.

Combine sugar, milk, corn syrup and margarine in large saucepan. Stir to combine; cook over medium heat until mixtures boils. Reduce heat and boil slowly for 2 minutes. Add orange juice and extract. Return to boil. Remove from heat and stir in half of the coconut.

Place cake layer on serving plate. Spoon $1/3$ of the mixture over the cake layer. After the mixture soaks into the cake layer, add second layer, spooning $1/3$ mixture over the layer. Add remaining coconut to the remaining orange mixture. Spoon on top and drizzle mixture over sides of cake.

PEACH COBBLER

Sara T. Dukes
Bartow, Georgia

YIELD: *8 to 10 servings*

½	cup butter
1	cup self-rising flour
1	cup sugar
1	cup milk
½	teaspoon lemon juice
¼	teaspoon ground cinnamon
4	cups peeled and cut into bite-size pieces fresh Georgia peaches
1	cup sugar
	Ice Cream, optional

Preheat oven to 375°.

Place butter in 2-quart baking dish. Bake until butter melts. Remove from oven and set aside.

While butter melts, combine flour, sugar, milk, lemon juice and cinnamon in a medium mixing bowl. Stir to combine; set aside.

Combine peaches and sugar in medium saucepan. Cook over medium heat until mixture boils. Remove from heat. Pour batter over melted butter. Spoon peach mixture over batter; do not stir. Bake for 40 minutes. Remove from oven. Serve topped with ice cream, if desired.

PEANUT BUTTER SQUARES

Donnie Walden
Powder Springs, Georgia

YIELD: *18 squares*

1	cup butter or margarine
1	cup crunchy peanut butter
2	cups graham cracker crumbs
2	cups sifted powdered sugar
1	6-ounce package of semi sweet chocolate chips
2	tablespoons shortening

Combine butter and peanut butter in a 2-quart glass bowl. Cover with paper towel and microwave on HIGH for 1 ½ minutes. Stir in graham cracker crumbs and powdered sugar. Press into a greased 11 x 7-inch glass baking dish.

Combine chocolate chips and shortening in a 2-cup liquid measuring cup; microwave on MEDIUM (50% power) for 2 minutes or until melted. Spread over peanut butter mixture. Cover and chill. Cut into squares.

PECAN KISS CAKES

YIELD: *about 8 dozen*

Juanita Boyd
Marietta, Georgia

4	egg whites, at room temperature
1 1/2	cups sugar
1	teaspoon vanilla extract
1	cup chopped Georgia pecans

Preheat oven to 250°.

Beat egg whites in a medium mixing bowl until foamy; add sugar, 2 tablespoons at a time, beating until stiff peaks form. Fold in vanilla and pecans.

Drop mixture by heaping teaspoonfuls 2 inches apart onto waxed paper-lined cookie sheets. Bake for 55 minutes. Remove from waxed paper and cool on wire racks. Store immediately in airtight containers.

VARIATIONS: Stir in 1 6-ounce package mini chocolate chips or 1/2 teaspoon peppermint extract or both!

PINEAPPLE PIE

YIELD: *1 extra serving size (9-inch) pie or 2 (8-inch) pies*

Don Peoples
Brunswick, Georgia

1	20-ounce can crushed pineapple, undrained
1	16-ounce carton sour cream
1	8-ounce frozen whipped topping, thawed
1	5-ounce package instant vanilla pudding mix
1	9-ounce graham cracker (extra serving size) pie crust OR 2 smaller crusts

Combine all ingredients except pie crust in large bowl. Stir until combined. Spoon into graham cracker pie crust. Refrigerate several hours or overnight.

Heavenly delights! No one can eat just one of these — they literally melt in your mouth.

These add variety to a tray of holiday cookies.

Don't try to make them on a humid or rainy day! They tend to get sticky and never crisp as they should.

Quick, easy and tasty.

Add sliced bananas, chopped maraschino cherries, chopped pecans, and you've got a banana split pie!

Light and delicious!

QUICK KEY LIME PIE

Minnie L. Tiller
Athens, Georgia

YIELD: *1 (8-inch) pie*

1	3-ounce package sugar-free lime flavor gelatin
1/4	cup boiling water
2	4-ounce containers key lime pie flavor whipped or light yogurt
1	8-ounce container reduced-fat frozen whipped topping, thawed
1	6-ounce reduced-fat graham cracker pie crust

Dissolve gelatin in boiling water; stirring well. In a large mixing bowl, combine gelatin and yogurt. Gently fold in whipped topping. Spoon into graham cracker crust and refrigerate several hours or overnight.

Very rich and chewy. Cool completely before cutting.

RASPBERRY BARS

Helga Darty
Ellenwood, Georgia

YIELD: *12 cookies*

2 1/4	cups all-purpose flour
1/4	teaspoon salt
1	cup sugar
1	cup softened butter
1	egg
1	cup chopped Georgia pecans
1	12-ounce jar raspberry preserves

Preheat oven to 350°.

Combine all ingredients except preserves in large bowl of electric mixer. Beat at low speed until mixture is crumbly. Set aside 1 1/2 cups mixture.

Press remaining crumb mixture on bottom of greased 8-inch baking pan. Spread preserves to within 1/2 inch of the edge of unbaked crumb mixture. Crumble remaining crumb mixture over preserves. Bake for 45 minutes or until top is lightly browned.

Cool completely; cut into small bars.

RICH AND DELICIOUS BANANA PUDDING

YIELD: *10 to 12 servings*

Mabel Hayes
Griffin, Georgia

1	14-ounce can sweetened condensed milk
1 ½	cup cold water
1	3 ½ -ounce package vanilla instant pudding and pie filling
1	pint heavy cream, whipped
1	12-ounce box vanilla wafers
3 - 4	bananas, sliced

Combine sweetened condensed milk, water and pudding mix. Beat until blended. Refrigerate 5-10 minutes or until thickened. Fold whipped cream into pudding mixture.

In a 2½-quart bowl layer pudding mixture, bananas and vanilla wafers. Repeat layering twice. Chill before serving.

Can be made the day before serving.

Substitutions to lighten up recipe: fat-free sweetened condensed milk, sugar-free pudding, fat-free whipped topping, reduced-fat vanilla wafers.

SOUR CREAM PECAN POUND CAKE

YIELD: *1 (10-inch) tube cake*

Gail Brown
Screven, Georgia

3	sticks butter, softened
3	cups sugar
6	eggs
3	cups cake flour
1	teaspoon baking powder
½	teaspoon salt
1	cup sour cream
1	cup finely chopped Georgia pecans
1	teaspoon vanilla extract
1	teaspoon lemon extract

Preheat oven to 350°.

Cream butter and sugar in large mixer bowl until light and fluffy. Add eggs, one at a time, beating well after each addition.

Combine flour, baking powder and salt. Add to creamed mixture, mixing well. Stir in sour cream, pecans and flavorings.

Pour batter into a greased and floured 10-inch tube pan. Bake for 1 hour or until wooden pick inserted in center comes out clean. Cool 10 minutes before removing from pan.

If you do not have cake flour, sift all-purpose flour 3 times and remove 1 tablespoon per cup.

Meet a neighbor. This pound cake would make a thoughtful and delicious "welcome to the neighborhood" gift.

This moist cake can be made with fresh or frozen strawberries.

STRAWBERRY CAKE WITH STRAWBERRY FROSTING

Hazel Davis
Duluth, Georgia

YIELD: *1 (13x9-inch) cake*

1	18.25-ounce package white cake mix
¾	cup cooking oil
1	3-ounce package strawberry flavor gelatin
4	eggs
1	8-ounce package frozen strawberries, thawed
	Strawberry Frosting

Preheat oven to 350°.

Combine cake mix, oil, gelatin and eggs in a large mixer bowl. Beat at medium speed of electric mixer for 3 minutes. Stir in strawberries. Beat one minute. Pour batter into a 13x9-inch baking pan or 3 (8-inch) round cake pans.

Bake for 35 minutes or until a wooden pick inserted in center comes out clean.

Cool. If making layers, remove from a pan and frost with Strawberry Frosting.

If making a sheet cake, frost in pan and cut into squares to serve.

Strawberry Frosting

1	stick butter or margarine, softened
1	1-pound box powdered sugar
½	cup thawed frozen strawberries

Cream butter and 1 cup powdered sugar in a medium mixer bowl. Add remainder of sugar and strawberries alternately, beating until mixture is light and fluffy.

STRAWBERRY-PINEAPPLE DESSERT

YIELD: *1 (13x9-inch) dessert*

Mary Jane McKee
Blairsville, Georgia

2	cups graham cracker crumbs
3	tablespoons sugar
1/4	cup melted butter
8	ounces fat-free cream cheese, softened
1/4	cup sugar
8	ounces fat-free frozen whipped topping, thawed
1	6-ounce sugar-free strawberry gelatin
1 1/4	cup boiling water
1	16-ounce package frozen unsweetened strawberries, thawed
1	20-ounce can crushed pineapple (including juice)

Preheat oven to 350°.

Mix graham cracker crumbs, sugar and butter. Press into bottom of 9x13-inch pan. Bake for 8 minutes. Remove from oven and cool completely.

Combine cream cheese and sugar in large mixer bowl. Mix well to combine. Gently stir in whipped topping. Spread mixture over cooled crust. Refrigerate 10 minutes.

Dissolve gelatin in boiling water; stir in strawberries and pineapple (including juice).

Pour over cream cheese layer and refrigerate overnight. Cut into squares to serve.

This would be great for serving a crowd — a family reunion or a church covered-dish supper.

SWEET POTATO PIE WITH PRALINE TOPPING

YIELD: *1 (9-inch) pie*

1	9-inch unbaked deep dish pie crust
3	large Georgia sweet potatoes, cooked, peeled and mashed
½	cup butter, melted
½	cup milk
1	teaspoon vanilla extract
2	eggs, beaten
1	cup firmly packed light brown sugar
¼	teaspoon salt
1½	teaspoons pumpkin pie spice
	Praline Topping

Preheat oven to 350°.

Prick bottom and sides of pie crust and bake 5 minutes. Remove from oven and set aside to cool.

Combine next 8 ingredients in large bowl; mix well. Pour mixture into prepared pie crust. Sprinkle Praline Topping over unbaked pie, if desired. Bake for 45 to 60 minutes or until pie is set in middle.

Cool on rack 15 minutes before serving.

Praline Topping

1	cup chopped Georgia pecans
¼	cup butter, melted
¼	cup firmly packed light brown sugar

Combine pecans, butter and brown sugar; stir with fork to make crumbly mixture.

TRADITIONAL PECAN PIE   (PICTURED ON PAGE 38)

YIELD: *1 (9-inch) pie*

Georgia Pecan
Commission

1	9-inch unbaked deep-dish pie crust
3	eggs, lightly beaten
1	cup sugar
1	cup light or dark corn syrup
1	tablespoon butter, melted
1	teaspoon vanilla extract
1½	cups Georgia pecan halves

Preheat oven to 375°.

Combine eggs, sugar, corn syrup, butter and vanilla in large mixing bowl. Mix well. Stir in pecans. Pour mixture into unbaked pie crust.

Bake for 55-60 minutes or until knife inserted halfway between center and edge of pie comes out clean. Cool on rack.

Nothing says "Southern cooking" Georgia-style like a Traditional Pecan Pie made from a fresh fall crop of Georgia pecans!

VANILLA ICE CREAM

YIELD: *3 quarts*

Mamie C. Conoly
Clayton, Georgia

2	14-ounce cans sweetened condensed milk
3	pints half-and-half
2	cups whipping cream
1	tablespoon vanilla extract

Mix ingredients and pour into freezer container of a 5-quart hand-turned or electric freezer. Freeze according to manufacturer's directions.

Set in a cool place for up to 3 hours to allow flavors to ripen.

If adding fruit, decrease half-and-half to 2 pints and add 2 cups crushed fruit.

Making homemade ice cream can bring back wonderful memories of warm summer nights and gathering on the porch. Did your family add fresh-picked fruit to your ice cream? Share your memories of making ice cream at home.

Index

Continued on next page

Recipe Contributors

Handy Substitution Guide

BAKING PRODUCTS

Baking Powder, 1 teaspoon . . . . .½ teaspoon cream of tarter plus ¼ teaspoon baking soda

Chocolate
    Semisweet, 1 ounce or 1 square . . . . .3 tablespoons cocoa plus 1 tablespoon sugar
    Unsweetened, 1 ounce or 1 square . . . . .3 tablespoons cocoa plus 1 tablespoon fat
    Chips, semisweet, 6-ounce bag . . . . .1 ounce unsweetened chocolate, 2 tablespoons fat plus ½ cup sugar

Cocoa, ¼ cup . . . . .1 ounce unsweetened chocolate, decrease fat in recipe by ½ tablespoon

Corn syrup, light, 1 cup . . . . .1 cup sugar plus ¼ cup water OR 1 cup honey

Cornmeal, self-rising, 1 cup .1 cup plain cornmeal, 1 ½ teaspoons baking powder plus ½ teaspoon salt

Cornstarch, 1 tablespoon . . . . .2 tablespoons all-purpose flour

Flour
    Cake, 1 cup sifted . . . . .1 cup minus 2 tablespoons all-purpose flour, sift 3 times
    Self-rising, 1 cup .1 cup all-purpose flour, plus 1 teaspoon baking powder plus ½ teaspoon salt

Sugar
    Brown, 1 cup firmly packed . . . . .1 cup granulated white sugar
    Powdered, 1 cup . . . . .1 cup sugar plus 1 tablespoon cornstarch (processed in food processor)
    Granulated . . . . .1 cup honey, decrease liquid in recipe by ¼ cup

EGG AND DAIRY PRODUCTS

Egg
1 large . . . . .2 egg yolks
1 egg white . . . . .2 tablespoons egg substitute

Milk
    Buttermilk, 1 cup . . . . .1 tablespoon vinegar OR lemon juice plus whole milk to make 1 cup (let stand
10 minutes)
    Sweetened condensed . . . . .Heat the following ingredients until sugar and butter dissolve: ⅓ cup plus 2
tablespoons evaporated milk, 1 cup sugar, 3 tablespoons butter

Sour cream, 1 cup . . . . .1 tablespoon lemon juice plus evaporated milk to equal 1 cup
OR 1 cup plain yogurt plus 3 tablespoons melted butter
Yogurt, 1 cup plain . . . . .1 cup buttermilk

FRUIT AND VEGETABLE PRODUCTS

Lemon
1 medium . . . . .2 to 3 tablespoons juice plus 2 teaspoons grated rind
Juice, 1 teaspoon . . . . $\frac{1}{2}$ teaspoon vinegar

Orange, 1 medium . . . . $\frac{1}{2}$ cup juice plus 2 tablespoons grated rind

Mushrooms, 1 pound fresh . . . . .1 8-ounce can sliced mushrooms, drained

Onion, chopped, 1 medium . . . . .1 tablespoon dried minced onion OR 1 teaspoon onion powder

Shallots, chopped, 3 tablespoons . . . . .2 tablespoons chopped onion plus 1 tablespoon chopped garlic

Tomatoes
    Fresh, chopped, 2 cups . . . . .1 16-ounce can, drained
    Tomato sauce, 2 cups . . . . $\frac{3}{4}$ cup tomato paste plus 1 cup water

MISCELLANEOUS PRODUCTS

Apple pie spice, 1 teaspoon . . . . $\frac{1}{2}$ teaspoon ground cinnamon plus 1/4 teaspoon ground cloves

Broth, beef or chicken, canned, 1 cup . . . . .1 bouillon cube dissolved in 1 cup boiling water

Garlic, 1 clove . . . . .1/8 teaspoon garlic powder or minced dried garlic

Herbs, fresh, chopped, 1 tablespoon . . . . .1 teaspoon dried herbs

Macaroni, uncooked, 2 cups (4 cups cooked) . . . . .8 ounces spaghetti, uncooked OR 4 cups fine egg noodles, uncooked

Mayonnaise, 1 cup, low-fat . . . . $\frac{1}{2}$ cup plain nonfat yogurt plus $\frac{1}{2}$ cup fat-free mayonnaise
OR 1 cup fat-free or reduced fat sour cream

Pumpkin pie spice, 1 teaspoon . . . . $\frac{1}{2}$ teaspoon ground cinnamon, $\frac{1}{4}$ teaspoon ground ginger, $\frac{1}{8}$ teaspoon
ground allspice plus $\frac{1}{8}$ teaspoon ground nutmeg

Vinegar, balsamic $\frac{1}{2}$ cup . . . . $\frac{1}{2}$ cup red wine vinegar plus $\frac{1}{2}$ teaspoon sugar

Worcestershire sauce, 1 teaspoon . . . . .1 teaspoon commercial steak sauce